S. Hrg. 113–222

STATE EFFICIENCY AND RENEWABLE PROGRAMS

HEARING

BEFORE THE

SUBCOMMITTEE ON ENERGY

OF THE

COMMITTEE ON
ENERGY AND NATURAL RESOURCES
UNITED STATES SENATE

ONE HUNDRED THIRTEENTH CONGRESS

SECOND SESSION

ON

LESSONS FROM STATE EFFICIENCY AND RENEWABLE PROGRAMS

FEBRUARY 12, 2014

Printed for the use of the
Committee on Energy and Natural Resources

U.S. GOVERNMENT PRINTING OFFICE

87–339 PDF   WASHINGTON : 2014

CONTENTS

STATEMENTS

STATE EFFICIENCY AND RENEWABLE PROGRAMS

WEDNESDAY, FEBRUARY 12, 2014

U.S. SENATE,
SUBCOMMITTEE ON ENERGY,
COMMITTEE ON ENERGY AND NATURAL RESOURCES,
Washington, DC.

The subcommittee met, pursuant to notice, at 2:50 p.m. in room SD–366, Dirksen Senate Office Building, Hon. Al Franken presiding.

OPENING STATEMENT OF HON. AL FRANKEN, U.S. SENATOR FROM MINNESOTA

Senator FRANKEN. Good afternoon everybody. The subcommittee will come to order.

My apologies to everyone who expected us to start 20 minutes ago. We're in the middle of some votes on the Floor. In fact, we're going to have to go back to that.

Everybody knows that this hearing is about what the states are doing on energy efficiency and renewable energy. I'm pleased that Ranking Member Risch and—is doing this with me. But we're going to start off with Senator Jeanne Shaheen who has been a leader in this area. In fact there's a bill called the Shaheen/Portman bill, maybe some of you have heard of it. I'm going to ask Senator Shaheen to deliver her statement and then we can move on to the work of the subcommittee.

Welcome, Senator, to the Energy Committee here.

STATEMENT OF HON. JEANNE SHAHEEN, U.S. SENATOR FROM NEW HAMPSHIRE

Senator SHAHEEN. Thank you very much, Chairman Franken.

I like this idea that you and I would do hearings, just the 2 of us. You know, I bet we could get a lot done in the Energy Committee if we did that.

Senator FRANKEN. We could. We'd probably get stuff passed unanimously.

[Laughter.]

Senator SHAHEEN. I think that would be a great idea.

Senator FRANKEN. OK, done.

[Gavel bangs.]

Senator FRANKEN. OK. I'm sorry. I didn't mean to do that.

Senator SHAHEEN. All kidding aside, I very much appreciate the opportunity to be here this afternoon. The opportunity to talk, not just about energy efficiency, but about the Energy Efficiency and

Industrial Competitiveness Act that Senator Rob Portman, who is also on the Energy Committee and I have been working on now for over 3 years.

I know that this hearing is to talk about how state practices can inform Federal policies. So I really want to begin by pointing out that I got excited about energy efficiency as a Governor when I realized we could retrofit state buildings in New Hampshire for energy efficiency. We could do it through performance contracts and not cost taxpayers any money and save, not only significant dollars, but also thousands of pounds of pollution in the state.

We also reached a settlement agreement with our largest utility that allowed us to set up a fund to encourage energy efficiency in the state. That has, by now, saved consumers over a billion dollars. So there are very real savings here. Energy efficiency is the cheapest, fastest way to deal with our energy needs. It is a win in terms of job creation, a win in terms of saving taxpayers money and a win on the environment.

I believe that's exactly what the Energy Efficiency and Industrial Competitiveness Act would provide to the Federal Government and to the business community. As I said, it's known as Shaheen/Portman. What it would do is really set a national energy efficiency strategy.

We have, today, been endorsed by about 260 different businesses and groups. Everything from the U.S. Chamber of Commerce to the National Association of Manufacturers, the Natural Resources Defense Council, the International Union of Painters and Allied Trades, just to name a few of the groups that have endorsed the bill.

According to the American Council for an Energy Efficient Economy, Shaheen/Portman, if it were passed this year, by 2025 would create 136,000 new jobs. By 2030 it would save consumers about $14 billion a year. It would lower CO_2 emissions and air pollution by the equivalent of taking 22 million cars off the road. So it really is a win/win/win.

There are provisions in the legislation that deal with the building sector which uses about 40 percent of our energy, that deal with the manufacturing sector which is the largest user of energy in terms of any sector of the economy and also the Federal Government which, as we all know, is the biggest user of energy in the country.

You may remember that the bill got to the Floor briefly in September before the government shutdown. We had to pull it because of negotiations around the shutdown. We are now working to include a number of amendments that had been cleared by the committee, bipartisan amendments, because the bill did pass the Energy committee back in September on a very strong bipartisan vote, 19 to 3.

Some of the examples of amendments that we are hoping to include in the reintroduced version is one around benchmarking that you will recognize since it's your amendment. That would require federally leased buildings to disclose their energy use data so we can continue to learn more about those buildings.

There's an amendment that would address Federal data centers and the amount of energy that those centers use. That's co-sponsored by Senator Risch, who is your ranking member on this subcommittee and Senator Udall.

Then there's another provision called the SAVE Act written by Senators Bennet and Isakson to improve the accuracy of mortgage underwriting by including energy efficiency as a factor in determining the value and affordability of the home.

Those are just 3 of about 10 amendments that we've been looking at to include in the bill. All of which have bipartisan support. Most of which have bipartisan sponsors.

So we believe that we're going to have a bill that's going to be even better to re-introduce. The positive thing, I believe, about this legislation is not just the savings that it would provide on energy, the savings on pollution, the job creation, but the fact that there is also a similar bill in the House that is supported by Representative McKinley, a Republican of West Virginia and Representative Welch, Democrat of Vermont. So it's got strong bipartisan support and the House leadership has expressed an interest in acting on it.

So I believe if we can get this legislation through the Senate that it has a great chance of passing and can make a real difference in terms of our energy use in this country.

So thank you very much, Mr. Chairman, for the opportunity to be here. I'm happy to provide any further information that the committee would like and to answer any questions.

Senator FRANKEN. Thank you, Senator. We are talking, as you mentioned, about what is done on the State level and you talked about getting excited this as a Governor. You are part of a small sorority of women who have been Governor and a United States Senator. How big is that sorority?

Senator SHAHEEN. That's a group of one. Thank you.

Senator FRANKEN. Oh, I didn't know that.

I did. I did.

[Laughter.]

Senator FRANKEN. But look, you and Senator Portman have done wonderful work on this very important bill, the Energy Savings and Industrial Competitiveness Act is exactly the kind of legislation that we need to make the energy sector more efficient. Obviously, I support the goals of your bill.

I know that we have some votes. Why don't you, if you want, you can go head down there. Tell them I'll be along shortly here.

Senator SHAHEEN. OK. If I could just add one more, 2 more points that I forgot that I think are important. That is that the legislation contains no mandates and it also provides no additional cost to the Federal Government, both of which, I think, are very important as we look to being able to pass this bill.

Senator FRANKEN. Yes and it's bipartisan and bicameral and all set to go.

Thank you, Senator.

Senator SHAHEEN. Thank you very much.

Senator FRANKEN. We—I guess I would like the witnesses to come and take their seats.

Senator SCHATZ. Mr. Chairman.

Senator FRANKEN. I would like the Senator from Hawaii to introduce one of our guests today.

STATEMENT OF HON. BRIAN SCHATZ, U.S. SENATOR FROM HAWAII

Senator SCHATZ. Thank you very much, Mr. Chairman. Thank you very much to all of the testifiers for making the trek to Washington, DC.

It's my great pleasure to introduce Mark Glick, the Administrator of the Hawaii State Energy Office and a good friend. Mark has been in this position since 2011 and has continued the good work of his predecessors in helping to implement and oversee the Hawaii Clean Energy Initiative which has some of the most aggressive renewable energy and efficiency goals in the Nation. Mark takes a holistic approach to these goals working very hard to ensure that the state, the private sector and the utility and the not for profit sector all benefit from the changes that are made in terms of jobs, economic development, environmental protection and energy security.

Mark knows that Hawaii's opportunities and challenges are tremendous. But he knows them as well as anyone. We're lucky to have him working tirelessly for our state. But he also has enormous experience from before he came to us serving as a Senior Advisor to the Texas Land Commissioner and working in the private sector.

Mark's testimony today will be a major benefit to the committee as it considers the lessons learned by our States in their pursuit of clean energy and economic opportunity.

Mr. Chairman, thank you again for the opportunity to introduce and invite Mark. I'm looking forward to this excellent and timely hearing that you've convened.

Senator FRANKEN. Thank you, Senator. Welcome, Mr. Glick.

We are going to unfortunately take a recess now. So I'm glad you all took your seats at the table and may want to visit with each other and discuss what you're doing in each of your States while we go and vote. I think we'll do the end of one vote and the beginning of another and then we'll come back and start.

So thank you, gentlemen.

[RECESS]

Senator FRANKEN. The subcommittee will come back to order. I will make my opening statement.

In the United States we produce a lot of energy and we use a lot of energy. Our energy consumption is about one fifth of the world's total. Although the majority of this energy is produced from fossil fuel sources, such as coal and natural gas, a rapidly growing portion comes from newly installed renewable energy. In fact 37 percent of new energy capacity in the U.S. last year came from renewable sources.

The Federal Government has played a large role in the growth of our domestic energy sector. New sources of energy including oil and gas in the Bakken region of North Dakota were made possible in large part by government support for research and development of hydraulic fracturing technology, in the case of the Bakken. So investing in research and development is critical and that's true for renewables and energy efficiency as well, but it's not enough. We also have to put into place forward thinking policies that will unleash the Nation's potential to deploy efficiency and renewable technologies.

Unfortunately it's been difficult for Congress to pass comprehensive clean energy legislation, even though this is prerequisite if we are going to win the global clean energy race.

In the meantime, many States which are really the laboratories of our democracy have gone forward with their own programs. States have established goals and mandates for renewable energy production as well as for increased energy efficiency of government and commercial buildings. These standards are stimulating the economy and creating new high skilled jobs.

My goal in this hearing is to learn more about some of the important energy programs underway in our States and to hear about what the Federal Government can do to better support them.

For example, a number of state and local governments have adopted policies that require benchmarking of energy and water use by large commercial buildings. This allows the owners of the buildings to explore ways to save on costs by improving energy efficiency. It's not just the owners that benefit. Of course this also helps businesses identify new markets and opportunities for energy efficiency. That's why we have a representative from a major energy service company here today to talk about the impact of some of these programs on their business model.

Developing and manufacturing the technology to retrofit these buildings will create jobs and contribute to economic growth in States across our country. This is something I've seen and encouraged in Minnesota. But being more efficient is only part of the story.

States have also supported new sources of renewable energy through renewable portfolio standards. These standards found in 30 States now incentivize renewable energy generation. Renewable energy producers and particularly the innovative startup companies need certainty for investment. These portfolio standards guarantee a market for their products and jobs for their employees.

These are just a few examples of the exciting programs that States have developed to grow and develop our energy sector. I hope to hear today about these programs so we can learn from them and potentially use them as models for Federal policy. I also invite the witnesses to talk about challenges that their States are facing in implementing these programs so that we may be able to identify how the Federal Government can help them overcome these challenges.

As chairman of this subcommittee I want to do everything in my power to ensure that the clean energy and energy efficiency programs we have across America are working as well as they possibly can.

So I'm very pleased that we have with us such an excellent panel of experts. Right now I would like to have you speak to the state of energy issues that we're considering today. We'll just go from your right to my right as if you're looking from the top. Underneath, never mind.

So with us today we have Steve Nadel, who is Executive Director of the American Council for an Energy Efficient Economy.

William E. Taylor, Director of the State Energy Conservation Office in Texas.

Mike Rothman, Commissioner of the Minnesota Department of Commerce.

Mark Glick, who Senator Schatz introduced, Administrator of the Department of Business, Economic Development and Tourism in the State of Hawaii.

Randy C. Clark, Senior Vice President and General Manager of NORESCO.

William A. Rodgers, Jr., CEO and President of GoodCents.

So we will start with you, Mr. Nadel and we'll go down the table. I'm going to be here so if any of you has to catch a plane or something, let me know, but otherwise, you know, take about 5 minutes, but whatever you really want.

I know you'll have to leave and I know you'll want to hear Mr. Glick.

If you want me to have Mr. Glick go before anybody, let me know because he flew in from Hawaii. I don't know if you know how far that is.

[Laughter.]

Senator FRANKEN. So if you need Mr. Glick to go because I know you want you.

Senator SCHATZ. Mr. Chairman, we're fine as it is. I'll just have to leave before 4.

Senator FRANKEN. OK.

Mr. Nadel.

STATEMENT OF STEVEN NADEL, EXECUTIVE DIRECTOR, AMERICAN COUNCIL FOR AN ENERGY EFFICIENT-ECONOMY (ACEEE)

Mr. NADEL. OK. Thank you very much, Chairman Franken and assembled staff. We very much appreciate your holding a hearing on this important topic.

As you noted, I'm the Executive Director of the American Council for an Energy Efficient Economy. We're a non-profit research and education organization that works on energy efficiency policies and programs.

Given the difficulties that we've had here in Washington reaching consensus on energy policy States are increasingly taking the lead. ACEEE has been working on state policy for more than a decade. We have assisted officials and organizations in more than half the States with policy and program development and implementation and are well known for our state energy efficiency policy data base with information on energy efficiency policies in each of the 50 States and for our annual State energy efficiency scorecard.

I included a summary of our scorecard, a summary map, on page 2 of my written testimony.

Based on our work with States it is apparent that most States are now taking at least some action to help consumers and businesses reduce their energy use and their energy bills and also to promote economic development through energy efficiency.

My written testimony describes 6 areas where States are working. In these brief oral comments I will just discuss 4 of them. I will leave the other 2 areas for some of the other witnesses, having seen their testimony.

The first area is utility programs and policies. Electric and gas utilities serve nearly every American household. They are generally regulated monopolies with an obligation to provide quality and reliable services to all customers at reasonable rates. Over the past several decades a substantial majority of States and utilities have recognized that programs that help utility customers to use energy more efficiently are less expensive per kilowatt/hour saved than the cost of generating a kilowatt/hour from a new power plant.

This is illustrated in Figure 2 on page 4 of my written testimony which shows that energy efficiency is typically half to a third of the cost of power from a new power plant.

Just to give a few examples.

Vermont is one of the leaders in utility sector energy efficiency programs. They have established an energy efficiency utility called Efficiency Vermont which operates energy efficiency programs in most of the State. Over the past decade Efficiency Vermont programs have reduced electricity use by about 12 percent, a figure that is increasing about 2 percent each year. So this is one of Vermont's largest industry resources.

In 2012 the program has provided the State's consumers and businesses with net economic benefits of over $100 million. That's the benefits minus the cost, still saving $102 million which is quite substantial for a State as small as Vermont. Independent study estimated a net gain of about 1900 job from those investments.

Energy efficiency creates jobs because designing, installing efficiency measures is generally more labor intensive than building and operating new power plants.

Another recent example of State leadership comes from Arkansas where the Public Service Commission established a series of rules to provide policy guidance guarding energy efficiency programs and how utilities would be paid for this work. It began with a set of quick start programs to gain experience and have now expanded to a full set of utility run programs.

In 2013 the neighboring States of Mississippi and Louisiana decided to begin their utility energy efficiency programs following what they called the Arkansas model.

Now utility regulation is primarily the province of States. However the Federal Government does provide technical assistance to States through the State and local energy efficiency action network which is a joint project of DOE and EPA. In addition I would note that utility sector energy efficiency programs are likely to be the lowest cost compliance option for meeting emission standards EPA is now preparing for existing power plants. Furthermore energy efficiency is the only compliance option that can save consumers money.

The second area I wanted to mention was building benchmarking disclosure. As we discussed earlier, as Senator Shaheen noted, Senator Franken, we thank you very much for the bill you've introduced on the topic. We are very glad to see that Senator Shaheen just announced that they will be incorporating that into their new amendment. So hopefully that will allow this to move forward along with some of the other important provisions in that bill.

Just to give a couple of examples.

The District of Columbia later this year will require all commercial and multifamily buildings over 50 thousand square feet to report benchmarking data. They will also eventually need to report their energy and water use to the district.

In Kansas, another example. A law was passed in 2003 requiring the disclosure of energy information for new homes. The energy rating law was amended in 2007 to move the time of disclosure from the time of closing to the time the house was being shown. The State has developed a standard energy efficiency checklist to be provided to potential buyers which compares the new homes features to the State's energy code guidelines. therefore, allows the consumers, the people who are buying these homes, to make informed choices.

We think an excellent way for the Federal Government to help the States is through passage of your bill, S. 1206, Senator Franken or passage of the new version of the Shaheen/Portman bill which now incorporates it.

Turning to a third area. Combined heat and power systems produce heat and electricity at the same time. By using the same system to produce both forms of energy waste is reduced and much higher efficiencies obtained.

For example with CHP systems combined efficiencies of 60 to 80 percent can be obtained, much better than the 30 percent efficiency of a typical existing power plant, even the 50 percent efficiency of the very best new plants.

Some States are leading the way to increase the cost effective use of CHP systems. I provide some specific examples from Mr. Taylor's State of Texas as well as from New Jersey.

Fourth and last I wanted to note that about building codes. Most States have building codes that specify construction practice to protect health and safety, reduce building energy use. In the case of energy use, national consensus organizations develop model codes and the States then adopt them.

As of this past October 40 States have adopted at least the 2009 model codes and that includes 14 States with more updated codes. So major progress is being made.

I'd also point out that working to have good implementation of the codes is also important. Idaho is an excellent example, as referred to my written testimony. Idaho has developed a plan that will achieve 90 percent compliance with their code by 2017 and is working with the Northwest Energy Efficiency Alliance to measure compliance in the residential sector. I understand that initial results are quite good.

Idaho also has an energy co-collaborative stakeholder group that helps train building officials, builders and other contractors.

The Federal Government has been working with model code organizations and there are a number of improvements on how the Federal Government can better work with and assist States in the Shaheen/Portman bill. So hopefully those will be adopted, when and if it reaches the Senate Floor.

In conclusion, I'd note that States are stepping out and leading energy efficiency efforts. It's a way to save energy, lower consumer bills and promote economic development. States can learn from each other to advance their efforts. The Federal Government can help by providing information on best practices, technical assistance, matching grants for innovative efforts and assistance in setting financing programs which some of the other witnesses will discuss.

The Federal Government can learn from successful State efforts and pass legislation such as Shaheen/Portman that builds on what States have done so far and helps them to do more in the future.

With that I conclude my testimony and look forward to your questions.

[The prepared statement of Mr. Nadel follows:]

PREPARED STATEMENT OF STEVEN NADEL, EXECUTIVE DIRECTOR, AMERICAN COUNCIL FOR AN ENERGY-EFFICIENT ECONOMY (ACEEE)

Summary

States are increasingly taking action to help consumers and businesses reduce their energy use and costs and promote economic development through energy efficiency. In this testimony I describe six areas where states are taking action: utility programs and policies, building benchmarking and disclosure, financing, state lead-by-example efforts, combined heat and power systems, and building codes. Most states have some good energy efficiency policies, and I provide specific examples in each area. States can learn from the practices of other states. The federal government can assist states in a variety of ways including sharing best practices, technical assistance, facilitating coordination among states, and providing challenge funding for innovative efforts. I make specific suggestions in the discussion of each program area. In addition, in light of the current propane crisis in the upper Midwest and Northeast, I briefly discuss how states can use energy efficiency to reduce demand for propane and fuel oil.

I conclude that states are stepping out and leading energy efficiency efforts in the United States. In most cases these have been bipartisan measures. The federal government can learn from specific state efforts, and perhaps also see that energy efficiency enjoys bipartisan support and may be one of the few areas where Congress can make progress this year. The Senate Energy Committee reported out the Shaheen-Portman Energy Savings and Industrial Competitiveness Act (S. 1392) on a strong bipartisan vote. Since then a variety of bipartisan amendments have been added, including several that build on successful state efforts and would help states do more. I hope this spirit of bipartisanship will spread to the full Senate and House and that the Shaheen-Portman bill will be enacted into law.

Introduction

My name is Steven Nadel, and I am the executive director of the American Council for an Energy-Efficient Economy (ACEEE), a nonprofit organization that acts as a catalyst for energy efficiency policies, programs, technologies, investments, and behavior. We were formed in 1980 by energy researchers and now work with an array of researchers, businesses, and national, state, and local policymakers. I have been personally involved in energy efficiency issues since the late 1970s and have testified multiple times before this committee and its subcommittees as well as before the House Energy and Commerce Committee.

ACEEE has been working on state policy for more than a decade. We have assisted officials and organizations in more than half the states with policy and program development and implementation. We have an online database with detailed information on policies in each of the states (http://aceee.org/sector/state-policy). We also publish an annual State Energy Efficiency Scorecard that ranks each of the states on 26 variables and assigns an overall score.[1] These rankings have motivated many governors—including those at the top and bottom of the rankings-to take action to improve their state's rank. To provide just one example, at his 2012 Energy Summit, Governor Phil Bryant of Mississippi pledged to improve his state's low ranking, and in 2013 Mississippi was one of the most improved states in our scorecard. A summary map from our 2013 state scorecard is provided on the next page. Details for each of the states can be found at http://aceee.org/state-policy/scorecard.

---

[1] A. Downs et al., The 2013 State Energy Efficiency Scorecard (Washington, DC: American Council for an Energy-Efficient Economy, 2013). http://aceee.org/research-report/e13k.

10

Figure 1.* Summary results of ACEEE 2013 State Energy Efficiency Scorecard

Based on our analysis of state policy over the past decade, we are happy to report that the majority of states have taken action to promote energy efficiency as a means of saving energy, lowering consumer bills, and promoting economic development. Furthermore, we find that the number of state energy efficiency programs and policies is increasing each year. State action and leadership on energy efficiency are particularly important given the difficulties Congress has had in reaching consensus on energy policy in recent years.

In this testimony I discuss six areas where states can lead, and have led, on energy efficiency, providing specific examples for each. These areas are:

1. Utility programs and policies
2. Building benchmarking and disclosure
3. Financing
4. State lead-by-example efforts
5. Combined heat and power systems
6. Building codes

In addition, given the propane crisis now facing the upper Midwest, I have been asked to briefly discuss strategies for using energy efficiency to reduce demand for propane and heating oil.

Areas of State Leadership

Utility Programs and Policies

Electric and gas utilities serve nearly every American household. They are generally regulated monopolies with an obligation to provide quality and reliable services to all customers at reasonable rates. Over the past several decades, a substantial majority of states and utilities have recognized that programs that help utility customers to use energy more efficiently are less expensive per kilowatt hour (kWh) saved than the cost of generating a kWh from a new power plant. For example, a forthcoming ACEEE report finds that in recent years energy efficiency programs have cost utilities on average about 3 cents per kWh saved,[2] which is about one half to one third the cost of power from a new power plant as shown in figure 2 below.

In 2012 (the last year for which data are available), American utilities invested over $7 billion in energy efficiency programs. Annual incremental savings from these programs totaled about 23 billion kWh per year, or enough energy to power over 2 million average American homes for a year.[3] These programs save money for consumers and businesses in two ways. First, participants in the programs receive a direct benefit: lower energy use reduces their energy bills. Second, because energy efficiency programs are less expensive per kWh than new power plants, all customers benefit from a reduced need for rate increases to pay for expensive new plants. In some cases, energy efficiency savings can also defer or eliminate the need for transmission and distribution upgrades, further reducing the need for rate increases.[4]

Figure 2. Cost per lifetime kWh of various electric resources. High-end range of coal includes 90 percent carbon capture and compression. PV stands for photovoltaics. IGCC stands for integrated gasification combined cycle, a technology that converts coal into a synthesis gas and produces steam. Source: Energy efficiency portfolio data from Molina 2014 (see footnote 2); all other data from Lazard 2013.[5]

Vermont is a leader in utility-sector energy efficiency programs. They have established an energy efficiency utility called Efficiency Vermont which operates energy efficiency programs in most of the state. Over the past decade, Efficiency Vermont's programs have reduced electricity use by about 12 percent, a figure that is increasing by about 2 percent each year. In 2012, according to an Efficiency Vermont estimate that has been verified by the state regulator, the programs provided the state's

---

*All figures have been retained in subcommittee files.
[2] M. Molina, Still the First Fuel: National Review of Energy Efficiency Cost of Saved Energy (draft title) (Washington, DC: ACEEE, forthcoming April 2014).
[3] Downs et al. 2013. See footnote 1
[4] Regulatory Assistance Project, U.S. Experience with Efficiency as a Transmission and Distribution Resource (Montpelier, VT: Regulatory Assistance Project, 2012). http://raponline.org/document/download/id/6120
[5] Lazard, Levelized Cost of Energy Analysis Version 7.0. (Washington, DC: Lazard, 2013). http://gallery.mailchimp.com/ce17780900c3d223633ecfa59/files/Lazard___Levelized___Cost___of___Energy___v7.0.1.pdf

consumers and businesses with net economic benefits of $102 million.[6] An independent study estimated a net gain of about 1,900 job-years from 2012 investments plus spending of the money saved as a result of efficiency measures installed in 2012.[7] Energy efficiency creates jobs because designing and installing efficiency measures is generally more labor-intensive than building and operating new power plants.

Another recent example of state leadership comes from Arkansas where the Public Service Commission established a series of rules to provide policy guidance regarding energy efficiency programs and how utilities would be paid for this work. Arkansas began with a set of quick-start programs to gain experience and now has expanded to a full set of utility-run programs, with a savings target in 2015 of 0.9 percent of sales from measures installed in 2015. In 2013, the neighboring states of Mississippi and Louisiana decided to begin utility energy efficiency programs using the Arkansas model.

Utility regulation is primarily the province of states. However, the federal government does provide technical assistance to states through the State and Local Energy Efficiency Action Network (SEE Action), a joint project of DOE and EPA. This program conducts studies on best practices that all states can use and also provides customized assistance when requested by states.

A more aggressive federal strategy would be to establish federal energy-saving targets for utilities. Twenty-six states have set such targets.[8] A forthcoming ACEEE study finds that most of these states are either exceeding, meeting, or close to meeting their targets.[9] Based on this record of success, Senator Markey has proposed federal targets in S. 1627.

BUILDING BENCHMARKING AND DISCLOSURE

A variety of states and cities have established policies to require benchmarking buildings' energy performance relative to similar buildings; in some cases they also require the disclosure of this information to potential purchasers or renters. Some policies apply just to public facilities, others to large properties (e.g., buildings with a floor area of 50,000 square feet or more), and others more broadly. Such policies allow building owners to identify inefficient buildings and target them for retrofits. Where disclosure is required, knowledge of building operating costs can inform the decisions of prospective purchasers and renters.

The District of Columbia and Kansas provide examples of what states can do. In the District of Columbia, by later this year all commercial and multifamily buildings over 50,000 square feet will be required to report benchmarking data to the District on a yearly basis. The EPA ENERGY STAR® Portfolio Manager is used to measure a building's energy performance. In the District, 266 buildings, representing 90 million square feet have taken the next step and been certified with the ENERGY STAR label. District buildings of more than 150,000 square feet were required to report their 2012 energy and water use to the District Department of the Environment prior to April 2013. The scope of the policy is set to expand in coming years and will ultimately include all commercial and multifamily buildings of more than 50,000 square feet.

In Kansas, a law was passed in 2003 requiring the disclosure of energy efficiency information for new homes (K.S.A. 66-1228). The state developed a standard reporting format for builders and sellers in which new homes' features are compared to the state's energy code guidelines. The energy rating law was amended in 2007 to move the time of disclosure from the time of closing to the time the house was being shown. A completed energy efficiency checklist must be made available to potential buyers.

The federal government can help state efforts in this area by providing technical assistance and perhaps some funding to help states and other market players get started. S. 1206, introduced by Senator Franken, will encourage and help states to do benchmarking and disclosure by (1) conducting a study on benchmarking and dis-

[6] Efficiency Vermont, 2012 Annual Report (Burlington, VT: Efficiency Vermont, 2013). http://www.efficiencyvermont.com/docs/about_efficiency_vermont/annual_reports/Efficiency-Vermont-Annual-Report-2012.pdf

[7] 7 Optimal Energy and Synapse Resource Economics, Economic Impacts of Energy Efficiency Investments in Vermont: Final Report (Rutland, VT: Optimal Energy, 2011). Appendix 5 in http://publicservice.vermont.gov/sites/psd/files/Pubs_Plans_Reports/State_Plans/Comp_Energy_Plan/2011/2011 percent20CEP_Appendixes percent5B1 percent5D.pdf. A job year is a full-time-equivalent (FTE) job for one year.

[8] Downs et al. 2013. See footnote 1. This scorecard lists 25 states; Connecticut is a more recent addition.

[9] A. Downs and C. Cui, EERS Progress Report (draft title) (Washington, DC: ACEEE, forthcoming March 2014).

closure best practices, (2) combining existing databases of benchmarking data to make it easier to compare and analyze data, and (3) establishing a small competitive grant program for utilities and their partners to make whole-building data available to building owners and help them benchmark the performance of their buildings. My understanding is that Senators Shaheen and Portman will be incorporating this bill into their larger Energy Savings and Industrial Competitiveness Act (S. 1392). We commend Senators Franken, Shaheen, and Portman for their efforts to develop this bill and move it forward.

Financing

Energy efficiency measures generally require an up-front cost but then pay back in terms of lower energy bills over several years. While some consumers and businesses have access to the capital needed to make these investments, consumers who lack the capital need financing to undertake energy-saving projects. Some building owners finance efficiency upgrades when they refinance their mortgages. While some banks are interested in financing specifically for energy efficiency upgrades, most are unfamiliar with such upgrades and so are not involved in this market. To facilitate the flow of private capital into this market, many states have partnered with banks and other lenders in a variety of ways to make financing widely available. Other states have set up their own financing and/or incentive programs. Two strong examples are Pennsylvania and Alaska.

Pennsylvania has offered the Keystone HELP program since 2006. The program is run out of the State Treasurer's office. AFC First Financial, an independent financial institution, originates the loans and completes the work through a network of approved in-state contractors. To date, more than 11,000 loans have been made totaling about $75 million. Capital was initially provided through the Treasurer. However in 2013 the Treasurer packaged and sold nearly 4,700 loans to investors, raising $31.3 million to replenish the capital available for new loans.

Alaska uses substantial state appropriations to fund energy efficiency incentive programs. The Home Energy Rebate Program uses $160 million in state funding appropriated in 2008, a major investment relative to the state's population, but an important one given the state's extreme climate and high heating bills. The program allows rebates of up to $10,000 based on improved efficiency and eligible receipts. Energy ratings are required before and after the home improvements. The program also provides expert advice on energy efficiency improvements for consumers and tracks their savings.

To take a few more examples, Texas has run a very successful "LoanStar" program for more than two decades. Tennessee has partnered with Pathway Lending, a small-business lending initiative that has grown into a statewide economic development lender, to provide low-interest energy efficiency loans to businesses. Nebraska has a Dollar and Energy Savings Loan program that has financed a range of projects covering all sectors. Connecticut's new "Green Bank" program is off to a good start, particularly with commercial PACE loans. (PACE is an acronym for Property Accessed Clean Energy, a financing system where the financing charges are included on property tax bills.) Hawaii has also started some interesting on-bill financing programs in the past few years, but I will let the witness on this panel from the Hawaii Energy Office discuss these.

The federal government can help with technical assistance and making capital available. The Federal Housing Administration is offering an Energy Savers loan program that some states are promoting. The federal government should also study the default rate for energy efficiency loans and for mortgages associated with such loans to provide improved information on the relative risk of various types of energy efficiency financing.

In addition, several relevant bills are pending before Congress. Senators Sanders, Wyden, and Murkowski introduced S. 1200 to expand the availability of residential financing. Congress can also make it easier to use home mortgages to improve a home's energy efficiency at the time of purchase. S. 1106 by Senators Bennet and Isakson introduces a variety of reforms in this regard. My understanding is that Senators Shaheen and Portman will incorporate this latter bill into S. 1392.

State Lead-by-Example Efforts

States can make their own buildings, fleets, and other facilities more energy efficient and thereby reduce their operating costs. Such efforts also set a good example that shows in-state businesses what they can do.

To take one instance, over the past decade Minnesota has shown its commitment to sustainable buildings by setting high performance standards and implementing integrated programs that design, manage, and improve building energy performance. The state has set a long-term goal of having a zero-carbon state building stock by 2030, and it offers a complementary benchmarking program to track energy use as well as a program to help implement retrofits. Minnesota also requires on-road vehicles owned by state departments to reduce gasoline consumption by 50 percent by 2015. Additionally, new on-road vehicles must have a fuel efficiency rating that exceeds 30 mpg for city and 35 mpg for highway.

In Mississippi, the Energy Sustainability and Development Act of 2013 requires all state agencies to report energy consumption or face penalties. Agencies work with the Mississippi Development Authority Energy and Natural Resources Division to develop energy management plans. The state has also set a goal of achieving 20 percent energy savings in public facilities by 2020 and has upgraded its energy codes for public and private buildings. Mississippi is also working to improve its fleet efficiency, requiring at least 75 percent of state vehicles to meet fuel economy standards of at least 40 mpg by mid-2014.

Likewise, Hawaii's lead-by-example program offers comprehensive energy efficiency services to state agencies. Aggressive policies underpin the program and include a benchmarking requirement that all state agencies evaluate energy efficiency in existing buildings of qualifying size and energy characteristics. Each agency sets benchmarks for these buildings using ENERGY STAR Portfolio Manager or a similar tool, and buildings must be retro-commissioned every five years.[10] In addition, new state buildings must meet LEED Silver standards. As a result of Hawaii's lead-by-example program, in 2011 total state agency electricity consumption was 4.6 percent below that of the 2005 baseline year.

Oklahoma also stands out in this area. Their lead-by-example efforts were a key factor in their being recognized as one of the most improved states in the ACEEE 2012 State Energy Efficiency Scorecard.

The federal government has been a leader in developing Energy Savings Performance Contracts (ESPC) that leverage private capital to upgrade federal buildings. While quite a few states have used this mechanism, some have not. The Department of Energy should step up its efforts to help these latter states establish their own ESPC programs.

Combined Heat and Power

Combined heat and power (CHP) systems produce both heat and electricity at the same time. By using the same system to produce both forms of energy, waste is reduced and much higher efficiencies can be obtained. For example, with CHP systems, combined efficiencies of 60 percent to 80 percent can be obtained, much better than the 30 percent efficiency of an average power plant or even the 50 percent efficiency of a new high-efficiency plant.

The growth of CHP has been slow due to a variety of barriers in some states, including overly stringent requirements to hook up to the electric grid, high backup power charges, and environmental regulations that fail to recognize the higher efficiency of CHP systems.

Some states are leading the way to increase the use of cost-effective CHP systems. For example, in May 2013, Texas House Bill 2049 became law, amending the state Utilities Code to allow owners of CHP units to sell excess electric power at retail prices to more than one purchaser of the CHP unit's thermal output. Owners of CHP units who do this are not subject to regulation as a retail electric utility. This new law should make it simpler for CHP operators to sell excess power and make investment in CHP more attractive.

After New Jersey was particularly hard hit by Hurricane Sandy in October 2012, the state began to look at CHP as protection against future extreme weather events. New Jersey previously had CHP incentive programs and had set a target of 1,500 megawatts (MW) of new CHP facilities by 2020. Following Sandy, the state decided to prioritize facilities such as hospitals, prisons, and wastewater treatment plants that would be most in need of power in the event of another Sandy-like scenario. New Jersey is now establishing new policies and programs to put these plans into effect.[11]

The federal government can encourage and help states to adopt policies that support cost-effective CHP systems. The joint DOE/EPA SEE Action program is one example. Federal tax incentives are also available for CHP systems meeting efficiency

[10] When a building is new, its various systems need to be tested and calibrated so they operate as designed, a process called commissioning. But systems get out of calibration and should be periodically retro-commissioned.
[11] M. Winka, "New Jersey's Clean Energy Program: Opportunities for CHP" (presentation to NGA Policy Academy on Industrial EE and CHP) (Trenton, NJ: New Jersey Board of Public Utilities, 2013). http://www.nga.org/files/live/sites/NGA/files/pdf/2013/1303PolicyAcademyWINKA.pdf .

thresholds, a program originally enacted in the Emergency Economic Stabilization Act of 2008.

Building Codes

Most states have building codes that specify construction practices to protect health and safety and reduce building energy use. In the case of energy use, national consensus organizations develop model codes (e.g., the American Society of Heating, Refrigerating and Air-Conditioning Engineers [ASHRAE] and the International Energy Conservation Code [IECC]). States generally adopt these model codes, which are typically updated every three years.

The American Recovery and Reinvestment Act of 2009 (ARRA) encouraged states to adopt the then most recent codes. Forty states plus the District of Columbia have either adopted at least one these codes or were on a clear path to adoption as of October 2013. Moreover, 14 states have adopted a code based on model codes published in 2010 or their equivalent. Of these, ten states updated both residential and commercial codes (California, Connecticut, Illinois, Iowa, Maryland, Massachusetts, New York, Rhode Island, Vermont, and Washington), and four states updated just commercial codes (Mississippi, North Carolina, Oregon, and Utah).

Working to improve compliance with the codes is also important. Idaho is a good example. They have developed a plan to achieve 90 percent compliance with their code by 2017, and the Idaho Energy Code Compliance Database for tracking compliance has been operational since June 2012. Idaho is working with the Northwest Energy Efficiency Alliance (a regional organization serving four northwestern states) to measure compliance in the residential sector, and the initial results are quite good. Idaho also has an energy code collaborative stakeholder group that trains building officials, builders, and other contractors.

The federal government has been working with the model code organizations and states for many years. DOE could improve these efforts by setting targets for new codes through a public process, providing increased technical assistance to code-setting organizations, and better assisting and encouraging states to adopt the latest codes and implement them well. Such provisions are contained in Title I of the Energy Savings and Industrial Competitiveness Act (S. 1392) which was reported out of the full Energy Committee last year. DOE assistance to states to help with code development and implementation is underfunded; we encourage this committee to work with the Appropriations Committee to rectify this situation.

Policies to Reduce Propane Use

The Energy Information Administration estimates that in 2013, about 0.50 quadrillion Btu ("quads") of propane were used in the residential sector, 0.15 quads in the commercial sector, and 0.05 quads for transportation. Much more was used in industry, but propane is combined with other fuels and not broken out.[12] Given the current propane shortage and the likelihood that the events that precipitated this shortage could happen again, it makes sense to improve the energy efficiency of propane-fired appliances and propane-heated buildings. Accelerated efficiency efforts for propane will not solve the current crisis, but they can help avert future crises.

In 2006 ACEEE published a study called Reducing Oil Use through Energy Efficiency: Opportunities Beyond Cars and Light Trucks.[13] As most propane came from oil, this study included many energy efficiency opportunities to reduce propane use, including more efficient propane-fired furnaces and water heaters, and improving the energy efficiency of propane-heated homes. For example, we found opportunities to reduce propane for home heating by about 38 percent, and opportunities to reduce propane for water heating by about 28 percent.

Many utilities offer energy efficiency programs for homes and businesses that use electricity and natural gas. But none offers programs for propane and fuel oil, and the fuel dealers are usually too small and undercapitalized to offer energy efficiency services. To address this gap, several states have begun programs to help residents using propane and oil. These programs are most common in the Northeast where a higher proportion of homes use oil and propane than in other regions.

For example, in addition to its electric efficiency program, Efficiency Vermont spends about $5 million per year on programs to save unregulated fuels including propane, oil, and wood. The funds come from Efficiency Vermont bids into the ISO-New England forward capacity market and from sales of emissions allowances under the regional greenhouse gas program. Most of the funds are used for the

[12] Energy Information Administration (EIA), 2014 Annual Energy Review, Early Release (Washington, DC: EIA, 2013). http://www.eia.gov/forecasts/aeo/er/.

[13] R.N. Elliott et al., Reducing Oil Use through Energy Efficiency: Opportunities Beyond Cars and Light Trucks (Washington, DC: ACEEE, 2006). http://aceee.org/research-report/e061.

Home Performance with ENERGY STAR residential retrofit service, which retrofitted about 1,300 homes using unregulated fuels in 2013. Smaller funding amounts serve the small business and commercial sectors.[14] An alternative funding source is illustrated by New York state, which has a very small tax on fuel oil. States could use a similar mechanism for propane, with the funds benefitting propane users.

The federal government could encourage and assist more states to implement energy efficiency programs for unregulated fuels through technical assistance, competitive grants, and financing.

Conclusion

States are stepping out and leading energy efficiency efforts in the United States as a way to save energy, lower consumer bills, and promote economic development. States can learn from each other to help advance their efforts. The federal government can help with information on best practices, technical assistance, matching grants for innovative efforts, and assistance in setting up financing programs. The federal government can also learn from successful state efforts and pass legislation such as the Shaheen-Portman bill (S. 1392) that builds on what states have done so far to help them do more in the future.

Good programs and policies are found in the majority of states, both blue and red. Energy efficiency has been a bipartisan effort at the state level, as it has been in the Senate Energy Committee. I hope this spirit of bipartisanship can spread to the full Senate and House.

This concludes my testimony. Thank you for the opportunity to present this information.

Senator FRANKEN. Thank you, Mr. Nadel.

We've been joined by the Ranking Member, Senator Risch of Idaho of which you were—the State which we just heard about the efficiency of your building codes. So thank you for joining us. We are—have been talking—we're just beginning the testimony because of the votes.

We started off with Senator Shaheen of Shaheen/Portman fame or Portman/Shaheen fame now. We're joined by the esteemed Senator from Ohio.

So I guess we'll continue our testimony with Mr. Taylor.Prepared Statement of William E. Taylor, Director, Texas State Energy Conservation Office, Arlington, VA

STATEMENT OF WILLIAM E. TAYLOR, DIRECTOR, TEXAS STATE ENERGY CONSERVATION OFFICE, ARLINGTON, VA

Mr. TAYLOR. Chairman Franken and Ranking Member Risch, my name is William E. "Dub" Taylor. I served as the Director of the Texas State Energy Conservation Office. Today I'm testifying on behalf of the National Association of State Energy Officials, known as NASEO, where I served as Vice Chairman.

I formally served as chairman as NASEO. Our Association includes all of the 56 State offices that represent energy issues in the State's territories and the District of Columbia. I'm pleased to be appearing before this subcommittee to discuss the activities within my own State, but also actions around the United States and finally how State actions in the energy arena can inform Federal policy and legislation.

You have my full written testimony and from that I would like to highlight 2 key areas.

First of all, select State actions.

Our Texas LoanSTAR revolving loan program has operated for 2 decades and has provided public entities over $390 million at low

---

[14] Scott Johnstone, Executive Director, Vermont Energy Investment Corp. (which runs Efficiency Vermont), email to Steven Nadel, February 6, 2014.

cost financing so they can implement energy and water efficiency improvements. LoanSTAR, which is also the nickname of our State, in this case stands for Loans to Save Taxes and Resources, a play on words. This program has made a major difference in bringing the utility costs down for public facilities thus allowing taxpayer dollars to be utilized for priority issues. We have hit our targets. The energy savings of $423 million have exceeded the costs and there has never been a loan default.

In addition to our own resources we've added funds from the American Recovery and Reinvestment Act to this program and this has made a significant difference allowing us to greatly expand the program. More recently Texas has begun to implement the Property Assessed Clean Energy or PACE Act in Texas which permits financing to be provided upfront allowing permanent energy and water efficiency improvements to be made by commercial and industrial businesses with repayment be a voluntary property assessment. To facilitate an orderly, consistent State wide approach to PACE design and implementation, we are working with a coalition of stakeholders including local governments, property owners, lenders, energy service companies and others. The results have been very positive.

I also want to highlight some of the actions being—taking place in other States.

Obviously you're also hearing today from Minnesota and Hawaii. We at NASEO attempt to work with the individual States and on a collective basis to provide good ideas and spread the successes.

Just like our LoanSTAR program almost 40 States have some form of energy financing programs.

In Alaska, for example, they established a $250 million Alaska energy efficiency revolving loan fund in 2010. The fund is available to finance energy efficiency improvements on public facilities throughout the State.

While most are revolving loan funds, we are beginning to see the development of so called green banks in the States.

In addition to financing, we've also seen a big increase in the development of comprehensive energy plans. NASEO has studied State actions and shared the best practices with all of our colleagues.

For example, in Idaho, the Governor's Office of Energy Resources which is the State Energy Office, coordinates energy planning with all State agencies, the Idaho PUC, the legislature, local elected officials and other stakeholders. Idaho has also participated in regional energy dialogs.

The second area I wanted to cover is what can the Federal Government do?

NASEO has been very pleased with the increased level of cooperation we are seeing from DOE under Secretary Moniz along with the new EPSA office led by Melanie Kenderdine, the Office of Electricity Delivery and Energy Reliability known as OE and the Office of Energy Efficiency and Renewable Energy. Coordination on energy emergencies through OE and EPSA has continued and has been necessary in light of this winter's propane issues and the aftermath of Super Storm Sandy in the Northeast. The extraordinary technical and analytical expertise of OE combined with the

State energy offices emergency planning, mitigation and response efforts is a Nation's first line of defense in limiting the health and safety impacts of energy supply emergencies, big and small that happen every year from weather, cyber and other market disruptions.

NASEO supports the continued next, on behalf of NASEO, I want to stress the support of certain legislation and Federal actions. NASEO supports the continued and expanded funding of the State Energy Program, SEP, and the Weatherization Assistance Program. These programs are a critical element of the State/Federal partnership. As you move toward FY'15 we hope the appropriations process will continue to recognize the import of these programs.

The most recent national laboratory study of SEP showed that for every Federal dollar invested almost $11 is leveraged from non-Federal sources and over $7 is saved where the State energy programs are involved. Senators Coons, Collins and Reed have proposed a bipartisan bill, S. 1213 to reauthorize SEP and Weatherization. NASEO strongly endorses S. 1213 and we had hoped it would have been included in the Shaheen/Portman bill, S. 1392.

Congress and the Administration can also help beyond the basic reauthorization by ensuring that the entire SEP appropriation go for the basic formula allocation.

NASEO also believes that the passage of the Energy Production Innovation Challenge, originally introduced as S. 1209 by Senators Warner, Manchin, Tester and Schatz, would be another opportunity for State/Federal cooperation. The bill would challenge States to develop new ideas and strategies for developing energy savings and improving energy productivity.

NASEO also supports the Sanders/Wyden/Murkowski Residential Energy Savings Act introduced as S. 1200. This bill would provide specific support in the residential sector by enabling people to borrow money at reasonable rates, improve the energy efficiency of their homes and pay back the loans.

These 3 bills would all complement the proposals contained in Shaheen/Portman and the McKinley/Welch H.R. 1616 bill in the House which NASEO also supports.

In addition, Chairman Franken's bills on building benchmarking, S. 1206 and the Local Energy Supply and Resiliency Act, S. 1205, that would encourage waste heat recovery systems are both common sense actions.

We would be happy—I'd be happy to respond to any questions. Thank you for the opportunity to testify.

[The prepared statement of Mr. Taylor follows:]

PREPARED STATEMENT OF WILLIAM E. TAYLOR, DIRECTOR, TEXAS STATE ENERGY CONSERVATION OFFICE, ARLINGTON, VA

Chairman Franken and Ranking Member Risch, my name is William E. "Dub" Taylor, and I serve as the Director of the Texas State Energy Conservation Office. Today, I am testifying on behalf of the National Association of State Energy Officials ("NASEO"), where I serve as the Vice-Chairman. I formerly served as Chairman of NASEO. Our association includes all the 56 energy offices from the states, territories and the District of Columbia. Our objective is to operate programs and develop and implement policies that improve our nation's energy position, and to diversify our energy portfolio. While the state energy offices are all in different places in state government, there are a common set of activities focused on energy and economic development, sensible energy efficiency and renewable energy policies, balanced portfolios and coordination with our peers.

I am pleased to be appearing before this Subcommittee to discuss the activities within my own state, but also actions around the United States, and finally how state actions in the energy arena can inform federal policy and legislation. I am very pleased to be appearing before you with my counterparts from Hawaii and Minnesota.

In my own state of Texas, we obviously have a large resource base in the oil and gas area. The shale revolution in my region, centered now on the Eagle Ford, has dramatically helped to improve our nation's energy position. As part of our commitment to a diverse resource base, we have implemented policies to facilitate the development of our Clean Renewable Energy Zone ("CREZ") transmission system upgrades, which has led to the multi-billion dollar development of wind resources in west Texas and high voltage electric transmission facilities to move those resources to the population centers further east. As the Subcommittee knows, our intrastate transmission system, ERCOT, is not regulated at FERC, but we believe our uniquely Texas system has been responding to changes in the energy marketplace. We certainly work closely with the large local governments in our state, such as Austin and San Antonio, which have helped expand renewable energy and energy efficiency opportunities.

I want to discuss a couple of programs in Texas in more detail. First, our LoanSTAR ("Loans to Save Taxes And Resources") energy and water revolving loan program has operated for two decades and has provided hundreds of millions of dollars in low-cost financing to public facilities to implement energy and water efficiency improvements. This program has made a major difference in bringing the utility costs down for public facilities, thus allowing taxpayer dollars to be utilized for priority issues. We have hit our targets. The energy savings have exceeded the costs and there has never been a loan default. In addition to our own resources, we added funds from the American Recovery and Reinvestment Act ("ARRA"), and this made a significant difference, allowing us to greatly expand the program. In addition, local governments in Texas have begun to implement a Commercial and Industrial PACE program, which permits financing to be provided up-front, and energy efficiency improvements to be made by businesses, while keeping payments manageable. My office has been working closely with the local governments to ensure uniformity and avoid needless duplication of tasks. The results have been positive.

While we proud Texans like to think we are the biggest and the best, just last week the state energy officials met in Washington, D.C. for our winter meeting. The energy directors all share very good information and we love to "steal" ideas from each other for good programs and policies. Of course, the overlay of the difficult situation in the propane market was discussed, and we are hopeful that situation will begin to ease, both on price and supply. Interestingly, Energy Secretary Moniz spoke to our group and forcefully made the case that he wanted better and more expanded partnerships with state and local governments. He indicated that he wanted our ideas for the newly developing Quadrennial Energy Review ("QER"), and we will be working together to supply those ideas to the Secretary. Some of the critical issues we discussed at the meeting revolve around interdependencies of our energy systems, resiliency, energy policy and environmental connections and how the states and the federal government can coordinate more effectively. After his speech to NASEO, the Secretary headed to Texas for meetings to discuss new developments and see firsthand the advances made in clean energy technology deployment, smart grid, infrastructure enhancements and responsible development of energy resources. He said in many ways, Texas is a perfect example of an all-of-the-above energy strategy as it leads the country in oil, gas and wind energy production.

I also want to take the opportunity to discuss some of the actions taking place in other states. Obviously, you are also hearing today from Minnesota and Hawaii. We at NASEO attempt to work with the individual states and on a collective basis to provide good ideas and spread the successes.

We have seen a big increase in the development of comprehensive state energy plans. NASEO has studied state actions and shared best practices with all of our colleagues. For example, in Idaho the Governor's Office of Energy Resources (the state energy office) coordinates energy planning with all state agencies, the Idaho PUC, legislatures, local elected officials and other stakeholders. Idaho has also participated in regional energy dialogues.

Just like our LoanSTAR program, almost 40 states have some form of energy financing programs. While most are revolving loan funds, we are beginning to see the development of so-called "Green Banks." Connecticut has implemented such a "Green Bank" and they are focusing on commercial PACE activities. Connecticut used $40 million to attract more then $180 million in private investment. Mark

Glick and the folks in Hawaii have a Green Bank that is developing solar energy programs. My colleagues in New York have announced the development and implementation of a new Green Bank, which is being capitalized up to $1 billion. One interesting example is in Nebraska, where they have coordinated with the local banks and credit unions on a program that has operated for 24 years. The Nebraska Dollar and Energy Savings Loan Program has supported 28,100 projects for a total of $301 million. The total defaults for that program over 24 years is less than $110,000. This program involves a lot of private dollars, but also some funds from the oil overcharge refunds and ARRA. Another interesting example is in Kansas, where that state has utilized an energy service company model and they have implemented energy efficiency measures in over 76 percent of the state governmental buildings. The Energy Service Performance Contracting ("ESPC") model is certainly being used across the country. A big focus on schools has helped in Idaho, where they completed 894 K-12 school building audits, followed by HVAC and control system tune-ups on 836 buildings and the installation of new energy software in 91 buildings. The federal government's ESPC program has also been expanding, which is a positive development. Last year in Oklahoma, Governor Fallin announced a new effort to increase the energy efficiency in state buildings by 20 percent by 2020. We are seeing a big expansion in energy financing programs throughout the country, and these are successful when they are coupled with public education activities so businesses and consumers see the value of actions in this area. In Georgia, they have ramped up performance contracting from $4.5 million to $80 million, just for state facilities. They have also lowered loan rates for local efficiency projects at water facilities, wastewater plants and landfills.

In Tennessee the state energy office is working closely with the Tennessee Valley Authority in a integrated resource planning process. The state has also developed a large, new education and outreach initiative to businesses, homeowners and government to expand the use of energy efficiency and renewable energy.

In Alaska, they established a $250 million Alaska Energy Efficiency Revolving Loan Fund in 2010. The fund is available to finance energy efficiency improvements on public facilities throughout the state. First, SEP funds were used to collect benchmarking data on approximately 1300 public facilities, plus an additional 100 university-owned buildings.

In Arizona, SEP funds have supported energy efficiency improvements in 33 school districts across the state. In addition, 57 small school districts are being helped to install solar photovoltaic systems.

In Michigan, over 25 loans and grants have been made through the Michigan Clean Energy Advanced Manufacturing program. One example has been the company that constructed a pilot scale biomass gasification center and an advanced manufacturing rapid prototyping center. They have also aggressively moved forward with an energy financing program.

In New Mexico, in November the utility commission approved a "whole home" energy efficiency program, as well as programs for low-income New Mexicans and home energy use reporting programs ($22.5 million).

In North Dakota, they have worked hard to expand industrial energy efficiency activities in partnership with North Dakota State University. They have also dramatically expanded educational outreach to farmers in order to increase their energy efficiency.

In Ohio, they have also focused on implementation of an Energy Efficiency Program for Manufacturers ("EEPM"), recognizing that reducing their costs keeps them more competitive.

In Louisiana, the state, working with Entergy has invested $14.7 million in 61 energy efficiency improvements that has resulted in $30 million in annual fuel savings. The SEP program has also supported their Home Energy Rebate Option Program ("HERO"), which has resulted in over 1,100 home retrofits and a 30 percent average increase in energy efficiency.

In South Dakota, they have implemented cost-effective energy efficiency projects in 55 state-owned building, totaling more than 7.4 million square feet of building space, saving substantial sums for taxpayers.

In Wisconsin they have implemented a statewide network of trained contractors to conduct energy use assessments and install energy efficiency products that help small business owners reduce their energy costs. They have developed a K-12 energy education program. They have also expanded a municipal alternative-fueled vehciles program.

What Can the Federal Government Do?

The Subcommittee has asked NASEO to provide our thinking on what the federal government can do to work with the states and to learn from experiences within the states. First of all, NASEO has been very pleased with the increased level of cooperation we are seeing from Secretary Moniz, the new EPSA Office led by Melanie Kenderdine, Pat Hoffman and the Office of Electricity Delivery and Energy Reliability ("OE"), David Danielson and the Energy Efficiency and Renewable Energy Office, Adam Sieminski at EIA and the Congressional and Intergovernmental Affairs Office. Coordination on energy emergencies through OE and EPSA has continued, and has been necessary in light of this winter's propane issues and the aftermath of Superstorm Sandy in the northeast. The extraordinary technical and analytical expertise of OE, combined with state energy offices' energy emergency planning, mitigation and response efforts, is our nation's first line of defense in limiting the health and safety impacts of energy supply emergencies—big and small—that happen every year from weather, cyber, and other market disruptions. Importantly, more rapid restoration of liquid fuel, natural gas, and electricity services also means a faster return to normal economic activity, which makes a real difference in communities across the country every year. Increasingly, energy supply disruptions are impacted by interdependencies among energy infrastructure (electric, gasoline, diesel) and other market sectors (e.g., rail, water, cyber, food supplies). The state-federal-private energy emergency and interdependencies efforts led by DOE and the states need your support and increased attention with regard to the great value they deliver to consumers and businesses and their relevance to the nation's economic and energy security. The states also continue to work with EPA on the voluntary Energy Star programs. We are working with HUD and DOE on manufactured housing standards and we certainly support efforts to incorporate energy costs in the appraisal process, both administratively at FHA and through legislation, such as the Bennet/Isakson bill (the "SAVE" Act). The "Tenant Star" bill (H.R. 2126) that recently passed the House Energy and Commerce Committee is another example of good legislation that would help address the split incentives between building owners and lessees. Now that the Congress has passed and the President has signed the new multi-year Farm bill (H.R. 2642), there is a real opportunity to expand such important programs as the Rural Energy for America Program ("REAP"), contained in the Energy Title, which would provide $50 million per year in mandatory funding for energy programs for farmers, ranchers and rural small businesses. The $889 million in mandatory funding in the Energy Title supports a variety of activities. In addition, the financing program for rural electric cooperatives—the Energy Efficiency and Loan Conservation Program—based on a South Carolina model would permit RUS to support up to $250 million in these zero-interest loans. NASEO believes these are all positive steps.

Continued and expanded funding for the State Energy Program "SEP") ($50 million in FY'14) and the Weatherization Assistance Program ($174 million in FY'14) is the first order of business. These programs are a critical element of a state-federal partnership. As you move towards FY'15, we hope the appropriations process will continue to recognize the import of these programs. The most recent national laboratory study of SEP showed that for every federal dollar invested, almost $11 is leveraged from non-federal sources and over $7 is saved where energy efficiency programs are involved. Senators' Coons, Collins and Reed have proposed a bipartisan bill (S. 1213) to reauthorize SEP and Weatherization. This bill has reduced authorization levels from past statutes, recognizes the flexibility provided through SEP and would update the Weatherization Program to move towards enhanced quality assurance and to permit the development of an innovation program which should allow volunteer organizations (such as Habitat for Humanity and Rebuilding Together) to expand their role. NASEO strongly endorses S. 1213, and we had hoped that it could have been included in the Shaheen-Portman bill (S. 1392). Congress and the Administration can also help beyond the basic reauthorization by ensuring that the entire SEP appropriation of $50 million go for the basic, formula allocation. Other proposals, as set forth below, could be used for competitive funding. A competitive allocation should not come out of the basic formula appropriation.

NASEO also believes that passage of the Energy Productivity Innovation Challenge ("EPIC"), originally introduced as S. 1209 by Senators' Warner, Manchin, Tester and Schatz, would be another opportunity for state-federal cooperation. The bill would challenge states to develop new ideas and strategies for developing energy savings and improving energy productivity. An estimate by my fellow panelist at ACEEE assumed that $8.40 in energy savings would be returned for every dollar invested. This would be a voluntary initiative that would allow states to lead the way.

NASEO also supports the Sanders, Wyden, Murkowski, Residential Energy Savings Act ("RESA"), introduced as S. 1200. This bill would provide specific support in the residential sector, by enabling people to borrow money at reasonable rates, improve the energy efficiency of their homes and pay back the loans. The U.S.

Treasury would provide funds to states who would loan the money out and eventually the Treasury would be paid back. Again, it is voluntary and flexible and would directly help residential consumers.

These three bills: a) reauthorization of SEP and WAP, with a new innovation fund and quality assurance provisions; b) EPIC; and c) RESA, would all complement the proposals contained in Shaheen-Portman (S. 1392) and the McKinley/Welch (H.R. 1616) bill in the House, which NASEO supports. In addition, Chairman Franken's bills on building benchmarking (S. 1206) and the Local Energy Supply and Resiliency Act (S. 1205), that would encourage waste heat recovery systems, are both common sense actions.

We would be happy to respond to any questions. Thank you for the opportunity to testify.

Senator FRANKEN. Thank you, Mr. Director. Your endorsement of my amendments and I'm sure Senator Portman was listening and Senator Shaheen will have copies of the testimony and we'll try to—I support those as well.

I'd like to welcome my friend, Mike Rothman, from Minnesota, Commissioner of Department of Commerce there. Thank you for making the trip. Please go ahead.

STATEMENT OF MIKE ROTHMAN, COMMISSIONER OF THE MINNESOTA DEPARTMENT OF COMMERCE

Mr. ROTHMAN. Chairman Franken, Ranking Member Risch and members of the committee, thank you for the opportunity to speak on the topic today of lessons from State efficiency and renewable programs.

As the Commissioner of the Minnesota Department of Commerce, I am one of the energy regulators for the State of Minnesota. With me today is Janet Strath, the Director of our State energy office. I want to applaud you, Mr. Chair, for holding this hearing. In addition to the written testimony I want to supplement and highlight some key important points.

We in Minnesota are honored to be recognized for our work in energy efficiency and renewable energy. I would like to repeat a few words of Governor Mark Dayton from his last State of the State speech and to say, "That we will not rest on our laurels, but rather we want to use our past achievements as springboards for Minnesota's next big leap toward a sustainable energy future."

Minnesota does not have, as you know, any of its own oil, natural gas or coal resources. We, however, do have a significant potential to capture energy efficiency and an abundance of wind and solar resources. Minnesotans recognize the imperative to transform our energy future toward a more sustainable, environmentally friendly and reliable energy system.

Today I want to share some of our great success stories.

Over the past several decades, through our Conservation Improvement Program, known as CIP, Minnesota utilities have invested hundreds of millions of dollars in improved energy efficiency. Minnesota's 2007 Next Generation Act expands upon energy efficiency and moved utilities toward an energy savings goal of 1.5 percent.

Energy efficiency is the first option for reducing energy use and minimizing related environmental concerns. In real terms, Minnesota's energy efficiency programs have avoided the need for about two 500 megawatt natural gas combined cycle plants.

In 2007 Minnesota also established the United States most aggressive renewable energy standard at the time. The standard requires the State's electric utilities obtain 25 percent of electric generation from renewable sources by 2025. The largest utility, Xcel, must meet a 30 percent standard by 2020.

I'm pleased to say that all electric utilities are on track to meet the goals with current and planned renewable power generation projects.

Minnesota has also established an ambitious statewide greenhouse gas reduction goal of 15 percent by 2015, 30 by 2025 and 80 percent by 2050.

Now this year Minnesota made several very important steps on the pathway of our renewable energy future. Surprisingly Minnesota has an abundance of solar energy, even in our northern climate. We're proud to point out that Minnesota has nearly almost the same solar capacity as Houston. To capitalize on this opportunity the State adopted a solar electricity standard to obtain 1.5 percent of retail electricity sales from solar to electricity by the end of 2020 and a 10-percent goal by 2030.

Minnesota also embarked on developing a value of solar rate as an alternative to enhanced distributive generation which is meant to achieve for utilities a price that reflects the true value of solar to the energy grid. We will be the first State in the Nation to implement a value of solar rate. We will be creating a model for the country.

We believe this will be a big leap for Minnesota's solar energy market. I can imagine the day when Minnesota has a strong solar energy component to diversify and strengthen our clean energy resources.

As background for your legislation.

Since 2004 all public buildings in Minnesota were evaluated using an innovative benchmarking tool. During that time sustainable building design guidelines were also developed for all public buildings that received a bond funds. In 2008 the guidelines expanded to a sustainable buildings 2030 program which significantly reduced carbon dioxide emissions. The 66 buildings designed under this program are predicted to save $5.24 million each.

On your legislation I want to congratulate you on passing the Rural Energy for America program. The REAP program is part of the Ag bill. It's a significant boost for the Ag community and Minnesota.

The Minnesota Department of Commerce supports your benchmarking bill, reflects the need for all building owners to easily understand how energy efficient their building are or are not.

We also support the Local Energy Supply and Resilience Act that promotes district heating, CHP. Minnesota, as you know, has a great success story in the St. Paul District Energy which supplies heating and cooling for Minnesota's capital complex as well as for much of the St. Paul downtown area.

I also want to express support for the State Energy Program and the Weatherization program. We are hopeful that Congress could head toward a more sustainable level for SEP of at least $230 million this coming year. The $50 million is certainly an important improvement, but a more sustainable level would be $75 million this coming year.

We also strongly support the WAP, Weatherization Assistance Program, the WAP program. The $174 million provided for Weatherization in fiscal year 2014 is a really good step in the right direction.

If you will indulge me for a minute I'd like to touch on the propane crisis in Minnesota.

Senator FRANKEN. That's a very important crisis right now. In fact, we were in near Faribault on a farm doing a roundtable or kind of a kitchen table event just this past weekend. So, please, I— you know, as much time as you want on that.

Not as much time, but go ahead.

Mr. ROTHMAN. I know you all have flights, so I will make it as short as possible.

But thank you, Senator Franken, for your strong leadership on the propane emergency.

Minnesota, like many other States, has been gripped by a prolonged shortage of propane. Over 15 percent of homes in rural Minnesota are heated with propane and many poultry and livestock farmers depend on propane to keep animals from freezing to death during our coldest winter in over 30 years. That's just as of today.

As you know, Governor Dayton has taken a number of emergency steps and I should say a lot of Governors have as well including declaring a state of peace time emergency. Minnesota and other States have experienced price shock of double and triple the normal retail prices. Dozens of homes throughout Minnesota have run out of fuel to heat their homes in sub zero weather over the last 2 or 3 years.

I strongly urge this subcommittee to focus on the causes of the propane crisis and to take actions to avert one from happening next year and the years after. Governor Dayton has written to the Administration and asked for additional funding this year for low income heating assistance, urged the Congress to take a look at that as well so that Minnesota can supplement its program.

I am pleased to join my colleagues here today. Energy efficiency and renewable energy are critical elements of all of our programs. It will help us achieve a clean energy future. As you indicated at the top to be able to achieve a global, clean energy race and win it.

Thank you, Mr. Chairman.

[The prepared statement of Mr. Rothman follows:]

PREPARED STATEMENT OF MIKE ROTHMAN, COMMISSIONER OF THE MINNESOTA DEPARTMENT OF COMMERCE

Chairman Franken and Members of this Committee, thank you for the opportunity to submit this statement for inclusion in the record of the hearing by the Senate Energy Subcommittee on February 12, 2014 entitled, "Lessons from state efficiency and renewable programs."

As the Commissioner of the Minnesota Department of Commerce, I am one of the energy regulators for the State of Minnesota. The Department's mission is to protect the public interest, advocate for Minnesota's consumers and ensure a strong, competitive and fair marketplace on a wide range of industries in Minnesota, including energy, telecommunications, insurance, banking, and securities, among others. The Division of Energy Resources, which includes our state energy office, is contained within the Department of Commerce.

From the outset, I want to applaud Senator Franken for holding this hearing and his leadership on energy efficiency and renewable energy. Today, I want to share some of Minnesota's successful and innovative programs in energy efficiency and renewable energy and how those programs relate to energy issues that concern the entire nation.

ENERGY EFFICIENCY

CONSERVATION IMPROVEMENT PROGRAM

Energy efficiency is a cost effective means to decrease the amount of energy used. Minnesota instituted substantial energy efficiency programs through its utilities in the early 1990s. In 2007, the Legislature required all electric and natural gas utilities to annually save 1.5 percent of their retail sales starting in 2010. While individual utility performance has varied, collectively Minnesota utilities exceeded the 1.5 percent requirement in 2011, the year of our most recent data. Incremental annual electric and gas savings (first year savings from newly installed energy efficiency measures) over 2010 and 2011 totaled approximately 1.8 million megawatt hours and 5.4 million dekatherms. Combined, these energy savings are equivalent to approximately 11.5 million BTUs-enough energy to heat, cool and power over 102,000 homes in Minnesota for one year. Energy savings through efficiency and conservation also have a sizeable impact on carbon emissions. As a result of the savings in 2010-2011, nearly two million tons of CO_2 emissions were avoided annually—equivalent to removing approximately 370,000 cars from the road for one year.

BUILDINGS—B3 AND SB2030

Minnesotans recognize the importance of understanding how our buildings work. Starting in 2004, all public buildings were evaluated using an innovative benchmarking tool. During that time, sustainable building design guidelines were also developed for all public buildings that received bond funds. In 2008, the guidelines expanded to become the Sustainable Buildings 2030 program -standards that significantly reduce carbon dioxide emissions by lowering energy use in new and substantially renovated buildings through cost effective, energy efficiency performance standards. The 40 buildings designed to the SB2030 Energy Standard so far are predicted to save approximately 250 million kBTUs per year-saving $3.25 million each year. These buildings are being built at the same cost as a building built to code.

The benchmarking tool-B3-has become the energy management tool used by all state agencies, allowing them to gauge which buildings are most cost effective to retrofit. Senator Franken's benchmarking bill reflects the need for all building owners to easily understand how their buildings are working-the Minnesota Department of Commerce supports the passage of this bill (S.1206—Benchmarking).

The Minnesota Department of Commerce also supports Senator Franken's bill (S. 1205—Local Energy Supply and Resiliency Act) that promotes district heating and cooling-Saint Paul District Energy supplies heating and cooling for the Capitol Complex as well as for much of the Saint Paul downtown area. In addition, last year the Minnesota Legislature passed legislation that allows waste heat recovery projects to count in utility efficiency programs.

RENEWABLE ENERGY

SOLAR ELECTRICITY STANDARD/RES

In 2013, the state adopted a solar electricity standard to obtain 1.5 percent of investor-owned utility retail electricity sales from solar electricity by the end of 2020. This solar standard is on top of Minnesota's Renewable Energy Standard passed in 2008, which requires all electric utilities in the state to generate at least 25 percent of their electricity from renewable energy resources 2025 and 30 percent by 2020 for the state's largest incumbent utility Xcel Energy (altogether about 27.5 percent by 2025). This will result in six-to-seven thousand megawatts of renewable capacity by 2025. All Minnesota utilities have complied with the standard to date-18 percent for Xcel Energy and 12 percent for all other utilities.

VALUE OF SOLAR TARIFF

The Legislature also directed my agency to establish a Value of Solar methodology. The methodology (developed by the Department and submitted to the state's Public Utilities Commission (PUC) at the end of January) included the value of energy and its delivery, generation capacity, transmission capacity, transmission and distribution line losses, and environmental value. We expect Value of Solar to provide an innovative alternative to net metering by providing fair compensation to solar customers while also allowing utilities to recover the reasonable costs of grid services. Investor-owned utilities may apply to the PUC for a Value of Solar Tariff that compensates customers through a credit (i.e., moving the netting from the meter to the bill) for the value to the utility, its customers, and the environment for operating distributed solar PV systems interconnected to the utility and operated by the customer primarily for meeting their own energy needs.

RENEWABLE ENERGY INTEGRATION STUDY

Minnesota utilities and transmission companies, in coordination with the Midcontinent Independent Transmission Service Operator (MISO) are conducting an engineering study on increasing the state's Renewable Energy Standard to 40 percent by 2030, and to higher proportions thereafter, while maintaining system reliability. The Commerce Department is directing the study; we appointed a Technical Review Committee comprised of individuals with experience and expertise in electric transmission system engineering, electric power system operations and renewable energy generation technology to review the study's methods, assumptions, ongoing work and preliminary results. The study will be completed in November 2014.

LINKS WITH FEDERAL PROGRAMS

STATE ENERGY PROGRAM

Much of the work that I have described has been completed utilizing resources from the U.S. State Energy Program (SEP). This federally-funded program has been instrumental in the last two decades as Minnesota has progressed in the deployment of its energy efficiency and renewable energy programs. The State Energy Program has provided the opportunity to have technical experts in energy efficiency and renewable energy technologies as those technologies have matured in the state. For example, these technical experts helped shape the Value of Solar tariff and are participating in the Renewable Energy Integration Study.

The State Energy Program also has a history of success working across all sectors of the economy and supporting cost-effective energy efficiency improvements. The last comprehensive study of the program by Oak Ridge National Lab showed that each federal dollar invested in the State Energy Program is leveraged by nearly $11 of state and private funds and results in more than $7 in annual energy savings. These SEP-supported projects and programs include a wide-range of activities, such as school and public building energy efficiency programs, energy efficiency financing activities, industrial and commercial programs, and energy efficiency for homeowners, and agricultural projects.

ENERGY ASSURANCE—PROPANE SITUATION

State Energy Program staff also leads the Commerce Department's energy assurance program, working with Homeland Security staff to ensure they have up-to-date information on Minnesota's energy system. This has been particularly important these past several weeks as a critical propane situation has developed in our state. Minnesota, like many other states, has been gripped by a prolonged shortage of propane. Over 15 percent of homes in rural Minnesota are heated with propane, and many poultry and livestock farmers depend on propane to keep animals from freezing during our coldest winter in 30 years.

Our State Energy Program and state-supported energy assurance efforts, in conjunction with the technical and analytical resources of DOE are our nation's first line of defense in limiting the health and safety impacts of energy supply emergencies-big and small-that happen every year from weather, cyber, and other market disruptions. Importantly, more rapid restoration of liquid fuel, natural gas, and electricity services also means a faster return to normal economic activity, which makes a real difference in communities across the country every year. Increasingly, energy supply disruptions are impacted by interdependencies among energy infrastructure (electric, gasoline, and diesel) and other market sectors (e.g., rail, water, cyber, food supplies). The state-federal-private energy emergency and interdependencies efforts led by DOE and the states need your support and elevation with regard to the great value they deliver to consumers and businesses and their relevance to the nation's economic and energy security.

In addition, we are doing all we can to provide assistance through the Low Income Home Energy Assistance Program (LIHEAP) during this emergency, but will need additional funds to get through the rest of the winter. Governor Dayton has called on the President to ask Congress to make more funding available and I join him in urging the members of this Committee to heed his call.

The Weatherization Assistance Program (WAP) has helped low-income families, seniors, veterans, and individuals with disabilities make lasting and cost-effective energy efficiency improvements to their homes and reduce the burden of high energy prices for more than three decades. To date, more than 7.4 million homes have been weatherized in the nation, providing as much as $450 in savings on a household's annual energy bill. Weatherization also supports thousands of high quality jobs. The National Association of State Community Services Programs estimates that there are approximately 10,000 highly skilled jobs in the weatherization network, with countless more supported in related businesses including materials suppliers, vendors, and manufacturers who make more than 90 percent of the products used in weatherization. The Weatherization Assistance Program has helped the construction industry and given a boost to American manufacturers and small businesses during challenging economic times. In addition, electric and gas utilities in many states depend on the WAP delivery network to carry out low-income residential efficiency initiatives, leveraging scarce resources and measurably increasing the impact of WAP in these states. As the program's funding has declined in recent years, both the state-level and private sector programs that rely on the WAP network and infrastructure have been impaired.

These two federal programs provide important links to ongoing state work. We strongly encourage you to restore funding for the Weatherization Assistance Program to pre-Recovery Act levels. The $174 million provided for Weatherization in FY'14 is a good step in the right direction. This equals the FY'11 funding level. We are hopeful that Congress could head towards a more sustainable level of at least $230 million this coming year. For SEP, the $50 million is certainly an improvement, but a more sustainable level, consistent with expanded responsibilities, would be $75 million this coming year.

We also support the Coons (D-DE), Collins (R-ME), Reed (D-RI) bill (S.1213) to reauthorize State Energy Program and Weatherization Assistance Program-two programs that are essential in helping states further energy efficiency and renewable energy at home.

In a letter to EPA Secretary McCarthy on December 16, 2013, Minnesota expressed its view on the proposed Greenhouse Gas Rules for existing sources that energy efficiency resource standards and renewable portfolio standards provide some of the most cost-effective options to reduce carbon pollution, reduce electricity costs to ratepayers, increase local economic activity, and create jobs. As noted above, Minnesota has a target of reducing energy use by 1.5 percent per year through energy efficiency measures and requires its electric utilities to generate 27.5 percent of their power from renewable sources by 2025. Carbon dioxide emissions savings from our Conservation Improvement Program have been increasing in recent years, reaching more than 800,000 tons in 2010. From 2005-2011, Minnesota reduced overall CO_2 emissions by 6.9 million tons, lowering its CO_2 rate by 17.5 percent, even while power generation increased slightly. Minnesota is committed to continuing its transformation of the generation mix for electric power and look to this federal rulemaking to help meet our commitments.

Minnesota is a national leader in the areas of energy efficiency and renewable energy. We continue to innovate to meet the growing need to find alternatives to fossil fuels while maintaining reliable energy services at affordable rates. We are eager to work closely with this Committee and Congress, as well as the Administration to achieve our shared goals.

Thank you, Chairman Franken and Members of this Committee, for the opportunity to submit this written statement.

I look forward to your questions.

Senator FRANKEN. Thank you, Mr. Commissioner.

Let me just make Senator Portman clear. Since I'm chairing this I'll ask questions last. I—Senator Schatz has to make a flight and Senator Risch has to go to the Floor to make a speech. So you're going to be asking the first questions, if you can stay.

I don't know if you're catching a flight.

Senator PORTMAN. I have to leave about 4:35.

Senator FRANKEN. Mr. Glick.

STATEMENT OF MARK GLICK, STATE ENERGY ADMINIS-TRATOR, DEPARTMENT OF BUSINESS, ECONOMIC DEVELOP-MENT & TOURISM, STATE OF HAWAII, HONOLULU, HI

Mr. GLICK. Good afternoon, Chairman Franken, Ranking Member Risch, members of the subcommittee and especially to our dear friend, Senator Schatz and quite an energy savvy Senator. Thank you for inviting me to testify before you today about Hawaii's innovative efficiency and renewable energy policies and to identify opportunities the Federal Government can take to support job creation and innovation at the State and local level.

My written testimony will—goes into more detail about all those issues, but and offers others examples of State leadership that might inform your deliberations featuring both Republican and Democratic State administrations. I'll be happy to address any questions you might have afterwards.

By deploying clean energy and attracting test bedded investments and innovation Hawaii is creating a clean energy cluster that is the leading source of new construction expenditures and green jobs. For example, distributed PV insulation accounted for 28.5 percent of all construction expenditures in Hawaii in 2012. As we reached second place in the Nation for solar PV insulations per capita.

Now at the heart of our energy and economic transformation is a bold policy agenda and coalition of energy stakeholders called the Hawaii Clean Energy Initiative starting with a partnership between the State and Department of Energy in 2008, the Hawaii legislature adopted the Nation's strongest renewable portfolio standard, RPS, in 2009 requiring 40 percent of our electricity to be generated from renewable sources by 2030.

Hawaii also adopted an energy efficiency portfolio standard in the same year requiring 43 hundred gigawatts of energy by 2030 to be reduced for power generation, roughly a 40 percent reduction in electricity use from 2007 levels.

Now we've made significant progress. When the 2013 figures are released we expect our renewable portfolio standard to be at 18 percent which means that we will have surpassed, by 3 percent, the 2015 interim goals 2 years early. Now in efficiency Hawaii has led the Nation for 2 years, consecutive years, in the value of our energy savings performance contracts.

I'm pleased to report that Hawaii has recently executed $167 million in 2 energy savings performance contracts, one that covers 12 airports statewide that will save at least $518 million over the next 20 years, and is the largest single performance contract by any single State agency in the Nation.

In 2013 Governor Abercrombie proposed and gained passage of S. 1087, a measure designed by the Hawaii State Energy Office, my office, that combines a rate reduction securitized bond structure and on-bill financing to enable broader base of utility customers to acquire a renewable energy system or energy efficiency device. When it's rolled out by year end, we expect the Green Energy Market Securitization, also known as GEMS program, to make energy improvements more affordable and accessible to Hawaii's underserved markets, such as low and moderate income homeowners, renters and non-profits.

Now for Hawaii connecting our grids is an essential ingredient in going beyond 40 percent renewable penetration. It's a commitment to exceed our Nation leading RPS made by Governor Abercrombie last year. A major policy achievement toward that end was passage of S. 2785 establishing a regulatory framework and financing structure for inter island transmission cable development. Analysis commissioned by the Hawaii State Energy Office with SEP funding and U.S. DOE support has demonstrated that unifying the Oahu and Maui grids with an undersea transmission cable will expand renewable penetration, lower electricity rates, enhance grid stability and reduce curtailment of renewable energy.

Now some of our suggestions for Federal action.

Since 2010 State energy program funding has provided Hawaii with $1.2 million helping us move the needle on our key metrics, RPS, EEPS, the Energy Efficiency Portfolio Standard and job growth. SEP has supported the State energy office's capability and leadership and regulatory proceedings, building efficiency systems and infrastructure analysis and energy assurance planning. It should continue to do so.

The U.S. State Energy Program is the only program administered by the U.S. Department of Energy that delivers cost shared formula funding directly to the States and allows each State to target funds to meet their needs. That flexibility has contributed to the program's long term success.

In conclusion the State of Hawaii strongly supports SEP. We urge Congress to continue your vigorous support for this engine of economic transformation.

Thank you for this opportunity to highlight Hawaii's clean energy agenda and offer suggestions on how future SEP funding can contribute to economic growth and innovation for Hawaii and the Nation.

[The prepared statement of Mr. Glick follows:]

PREPARED STATEMENT OF MARK GLICK, STATE ENERGY ADMINISTRATOR, DEPARTMENT OF BUSINESS, ECONOMIC DEVELOPMENT & TOURISM, STATE OF HAWAII, HONOLULU, HI

Good afternoon, Chairman Franken, and Members of the Subcommittee. Thank you for inviting me to testify before you today about Hawaii's innovative efficiency and renewable energy policies, and to identify opportunities the federal government can take to support job creation and innovation at the state and local level. I will also provide some other examples of state leadership that might inform your deliberations.

Hawaii's commitment to a clean energy future is propelling Hawaii into national leadership for renewable energy installations and energy efficiency measures. Energy transformation is a key component of the the HI Growth Initiative; our State's economic development strategy to create high growth, high wage jobs. By deploying clean energy and attracting test bed investments and innovation, Hawaii is creating a clean energy cluster that is a leading source of new construction expenditures and green jobs. This is growing our economy and diversifying our business base away from a heavy reliance on the tourism sector. For example, distributed PV installations accounted for 28.5 percent of all construction expenditures in Hawaii in 2012 as we reached second place in the nation for solar PV installations per capita. Hawaii is second in the U.S. for cumulative installed PV capacity per capita in 2012, according to the Interstate Renewable Energy Council, and also second for solar PV capacity installed in 2012, according to Environment America Research. We happen to be the most isolated population center in the world, 2,500 miles from the U.S. West Coast, with oil imports accounting for 74 percent of our electrical production in 2013 at a cost of $4.5 billion. Averaging 34-cents per kilowatt hour, Hawaii has the highest electricity rates in the nation, more than three times higher than the national average. Hawaii's clean energy policies are designed to transform the most oil dependent state in the nation to a national model for job creation, industrial transformation, environmental compliance, and technological innovation.

At the heart of the transformation is a bold policy agenda and coalition of energy stakeholders called the Hawaii Clean Energy Initiative. Initiated by a Memorandum of Understanding ("MOU") between the State and the U.S. Department of Energy in 2008, the Hawaii Legislature adopted a Renewable Portfolio Standard ("RPS") in 2009 requiring 40 percent of our electricity to be generated from renewable energy by 2030. Hawaii also adopted an Energy Efficiency Portfolio Standard ("EEPS") in the same year to reduce electricity use by 4,300 gigawatt-hours ("GWh") by 2030, roughly a 40 percent reduction in electricity use from 2007 levels.

In the six years since that MOU, we have made significant progress. When 2013 figures are released in a couple of months, we expect our Renewable Portfolio Standard to be at 18 percent, which means we will have surpassed the 2015 interim goal two years early.

In efficiency, Hawaii has led the nation for two consecutive years in the per capita value of our energy performance contracts. Our state has committed to the Clinton Global Initiative-CGI America to more than double Hawaii's existing energy savings performance contracting investments by State and County Agencies by 2015. As a partner in the U.S. Department of Energy's Performance Contracting Accelerator Program, Hawaii has also pledged to execute an additional $100 million in performance contracting projects by the close of 2016. These are not empty pledges. I'm pleased to report that Hawaii has recently executed $167.4 million in energy savings performance contracts featuring two state agencies. One covers 33 buildings that will save $28 million over the 20-year contract term. A second contract covers 12 airports statewide that will save at least $518 million over the next 20 years and is the largest single performance contract by a single state agency in the nation.

In 2013, Governor Neil Abercrombie also established the State's first energy policy directives and dedicated the State to move the needle even further when he announced that Hawaii is going beyond 40 percent for renewables at the State's annual energy summit last year, the Asia Pacific Clean Energy Summit and Expo. Hawaii's energy policy also encourages full use of our diverse, abundant indigenous natural resources, such as solar, wind, geothermal, biomass, and hydro, each which compete favorably with the avoided cost of oil. Please go to energy.hawaii.gov for complete information on Hawaii's energy agenda and online clean energy tools.

Our early success has brought unexpected challenges for our six isolated, island grid networks. On Oahu, our major population center, 25 percent of circuits are beyond the 100 percent of minimum daytime load. Hawaii Island has 46 percent renewable penetration and at certain times of the day exceeds 100 percent of minimum daytime load. This translates to something that mainland interconnected grids rarely experience, curtailment of excess renewable energy on a regular basis, and in some cases grid instability on a system level.

We have called upon the most qualified subject matter experts in the nation to help us craft unprecedented solutions for unprecedented challenges in clean energy deployment. Our mantra is to focus on high impact solutions and leverage funding and other resources to build the solutions for a new energy ecosystem. States cannot do it alone.

State Energy Program ("SEP") funding has provided Hawaii with $1.2 million since 2010, helping us move the needle on our key metrics: RPS, EEPS, and job growth. SEP has supported the State Energy Office's capability and leadership in regulatory proceedings, building efficiency, systems and infrastructure analysis, and energy assurance planning. Federal collaborations and funding have been and will continue to be critical ingredients in our success.

In 2013, Governor Abercrombie proposed and gained passage of SB 1087, a measure designed by the Hawaii State Energy Office that combines a rate-reduction securitized bond structure and on-bill financing to enable a broader base of electric utility customers to acquire a renewable energy system or energy efficiency device.

We call this "GEMS," for Green Energy Market Securitization and we're using SEP funding to implement what is potentially a national model. When it is rolled out by year end, we expect GEMS to make energy improvements more affordable and accessible to Hawaii's underserved markets, such as low- to moderate-income homeowners, renters and nonprofits.

SEP can help Hawaii and all other states with our increasing load of unfinished business. Building a 21st century grid is a must. In stretching the limits of what utilities can and should do, state energy offices, often with the coordination of the National Association of State Energy Officials ("NASEO"), can provide analysis, planning and regulatory support to fill the gaps. Smart technologies, such as advanced metering infrastructure and energy storage, are critical near term solutions to improving customer choice and widely deploying demand response.

For Hawaii, connecting our grids is an essential ingredient in going beyond 40 percent renewable penetration. A major policy achievement in 2012 was passage of SB 2785, establishing a regulatory framework and financing structure for inter-island transmission cable development. Analysis commissioned by the Hawaii State Energy Office, with SEP and U.S. DOE support, has demonstrated that unifying the Oahu and Maui grids with an undersea transmission cable will expand renewable penetration, lower rates, enhance grid stability and reduce curtailment of renewable energy. This analysis is helping inform decisions soon to be made by the Hawaii Public Utilities Commission on next steps.

SEP funding can also be effectively used, as it has been in Hawaii, to build and update a suite of online tools that provide developers, investors and policy makers with assistance in clean energy project permitting, interactive resource data, and GIS mapping. We note that competitive SEP funding is useful, but increasing the formula funding offers greater flexibility for program design and implementation.

Clean energy has propelled Hawaii into one of the world's leading test beds for energy innovation. Our isolated, island setting has attracted entrepreneurs from around the world, looking to develop, test and prove emerging technologies and strategies before going to market. By leveraging state funding sources with federal SEP, we plan on seeding an innovation ecosystem to spur the development of clean energy solutions while also creating high-wage jobs and economic opportunities for the people of Hawaii.

Other State Examples

Like my colleagues appearing today from Minnesota and Texas, I am pleased to note that all the states have programs that we each learn from. We also believe that these examples can assist you as you consider options for federal action.

For example, in Arkansas they have developed a loan-loss reserve financing program through the utility bills. This on-bill financing program is intended to address the needs of residential customers. Like many other states, Arkansas has also targeted multi-family housing for energy efficiency services— low-income homes are a special problem since the percentage of their income used for energy costs is so high.

In California, the voters approved a $2.5 billion California Clean Energy Jobs Act, especially targeting schools and other public buildings. They have also developed a program for clean transportation infrastructure and energy -related R&D investments at a level of $240 million annually. The state uses their SEP funds in the development and implementation of building codes and standards.

Colorado has instituted large new energy efficiency and renewable energy programs in the past few years. They are moving towards their targets of 5 percent reduction in peak electricity demand by 2018 and 30 percent of electricity coming from renewable energy by 2020. The state is estimating that this effort will add $4.3 billion to the state's economy and 33,000 jobs.

In Kentucky, they have taken the lead in promoting "zero net energy" ("ZNE") schools. They have now constructed 10 schools under this program, and they are finding that the initial costs of ZNE schools is comparable to less energy-efficient schools. This is really a "no-brainer".

In Massachusetts, my colleagues have aggressively promoted energy efficiency, solar development and greenhouse gas emission reduction targets, while maintaining double digit clean energy industry growth. They recently began to implement a $40 million program of community self-resilience associated with power outages caused by severe weather and climate change.

In New England, the governors of Connecticut, Massachusetts, Maine, New Hampshire, Rhode Island and Vermont signed a regional infrastructure statement that commits them to develop a reliable, affordable and diverse energy portfolio. Working with the regional utilities they are focusing on expanding energy efficiency programs and renewable energy use, while also developing new natural gas and electric transmission capacity.

In Oregon, the state has helped fund more than $11 million of projects in 60 school districts, including lighting upgrades, window replacements, HVAC improvements and biomass boiler installations. They are also implementing a program to convert 20 percent of all public and private fleets to alternative fuels. Pennsylvania has joined other states in promoting alternative fuels.

Pennsylvania has contributed $20 million in incremental cost incentives for the purchase or retrofit of heavy duty natural gas vehicles. They have also deployed charging stations at all the rest stops on the Pennsylvania Turnpike. Whether utilizing ethanol, biodiesel, natural gas or electric vehicles, the states are pushing to diversify the fuels used within the transportation sector.

In Rhode Island they have implemented a partnership to achieve 20 percent energy use reductions in 100 public facilities by 2016. They have also targeted new combined heat and power ("CHP") incentives that has already resulted in a new 12.5 MW project that reduced electricity use by 80 percent.

In Vermont, they have implemented a variety of renewable energy and energy efficiency projects for schools, communities and businesses, ranging from a biogas cogeneration project, a 12 MW wind plant and a 300 kW PV system.

In Washington, the state energy office announced the award of over $14 million to financial institutions as seed funding to help individuals and companies finance residential and commercial building energy efficiency retrofits and renewable energy installations. The Governor created 5 clean energy loans funds to stimulate economic development in the clean energy sector, and this is the first installment.

In West Virginia they have initiated an extensive energy planning process looking at all resources, both on the supply side and the demand side. This state is also trying to target the commercial/industrial sector through partnerships with the West Virginia University Industrial Assessment Center and the NIST-supported Manufacturing Extension Partnership.

Suggestions for Federal Action

The U.S. State Energy Program is the only program administered by the U.S. Department of Energy that delivers cost-shared, formula funding directly to the states, and allows each state to target funds to meet their needs. When Congress established SEP, it recognized that states were in the best position to understand their energy policy and program needs and opportunities. This flexibility is what has resulted in the program's track record of success. SEP is used by Hawaii, and all the states, to catalyze new energy business opportunities, reduce market barriers to energy efficiency and other alternatives, and support our governor's and legislature in the kind of energy planning and policy development that has transformed the energy sector over the past five years. SEP funding provided the seed funding and linkage to DOE that made the Hawaii Clean Energy Initiative possible. Similarly, the foundation for Hawaii's now successful ESPC program was laid using flexible SEP funding to develop public-private partnerships and technical assistance over a period of years—unlocking energy savings in the public buildings sector. This allowed our state to further advance ESPC when we recently partnered with DOE on the ESPC accelerator.

Conclusion

In conclusion, the State of Hawaii strongly supports SEP and we urge Congress to continue to provide your vigorous support to this engine for economic transformation.

Thank you for this opportunity to highlight Hawaii's clean energy leadership and offer suggestions on how future SEP funding can contribute to economic growth and innovation for Hawaii and the nation. As noted in Mr. Taylor's testimony, we also support enactment of the Shaheen/Portman bill (S. 1392), the SEP/Weatherization reauthorization bill (S. 1213), the Energy Productivity Innovation Challenge (S. 1209), the Residential Energy Savings Act (S. 1200), as well as Chairman Franken's legislation on building benchmarking (S. 1206) and the Local Energy Supply and Resiliency Act (S. 1205).

Senator FRANKEN. Thank you, Mr. Glick. I think as everyone realizes Hawaii is a little isolated and renewable energy is a big piece of that portfolio. I think your electricity costs are about 3 times out of the average, right?

Mr. GLICK. That's correct.

Senator FRANKEN. So, thank you for your testimony. Thank you for mentioning your great work with energy saving performance contracts which brings us to Mr. Clark, who is the Head—who is the Senior Vice President and General Manager of an energy service company.

Please, Mr. Clark.

STATEMENT OF RANDALL R. CLARK, SENIOR VICE PRESIDENT, NORESCO

Mr. CLARK. Thank you, Chairman Ranken or Chairman Franken, Ranking Member Risch and the subcommittee. Thank you for inviting me to testify.

Senator FRANKEN. I like that, by the way.

[Laughter.]

Senator FRANKEN. That was good.

Mr. CLARK. Regarding the role private sector plays in advancing State energy efficiency. I am Randy Clark, as you mentioned, Senior Vice President of NORESCO, one of the largest energy service companies in the United States. We are part of United Technologies Corporation, a leading provider to the aerospace and building industries employing 220,000 people globally and 90 thousand people in the United States.

NORESCO specializes in developing and implementing energy saving performance contracts, also known as ESPCs, for government and institutional clients spanning the Federal, State and municipal sectors. In my role at NORESCO I manage the performance contracting business with State agencies, local governments, school districts, universities and health care institutions. Today I will discuss how this private sector contracting mechanism provides a cost effective pathway toward reducing building energy use, lowering costs and reducing greenhouse gas emissions.

Under an ESPC a private sector company like NORESCO installs new energy efficient equipment at no upfront capital cost to the building owner. At its most basic an ESPC converts the money a building owner currently spends on wasted energy into a payment stream that finances the energy savings capital improvements in the facility. The building owner repays this investment over time using the utility savings.

The energy service company will measure and guarantee these savings and private sector financiers provide the capital. Under the contract the building owner never pays more than they would have paid for utilities if they had not entered into the ESPC. States are increasingly turning to ESPCs to achieve cost effective energy efficiency.

In 2011 Minnesota enacted legislation allowing State agencies to enter into ESPCs. The State created the Office of Guaranteed Energy Savings Programs to help pre-qualify energy savings companies on behalf of State agencies and to provide technical and financial assistance and oversight in the implementation of projects. Over 30 States have authorized ESPC programs and the energy service company market is estimated to exceed $5 billion annually. Regional benefits include local job creation of approximately 95 direct jobs and 114 indirect jobs for every $10 millions of investment.

Despite the benefits of utilizing an ESPC the mechanism is under utilized by State and local governments. The barriers to increased use are difficult to quantify, but stem from the fact that performance contracting is different from traditional procurements for government and institutions. Additionally, many ESPC projects are financed with long term, tax exempt leases or bonds. With increased uncertainty around State and local tax revenues since the economic downturn building owners are reluctant to incur debt related to building improvements even when these building improvements are funded through energy savings.

Some States are taking steps to address these barriers.

The State of Delaware created the Sustainable Energy Utility, the SEU, to create a market for energy efficiency for buildings in the State. The SEU issues tax exempt debt on behalf of public entities in the State in order to fund the investment in building infrastructure. The SEU issued $70 million of bonds in 2011 and has a number of comprehensive energy efficiency projects completed or in the final stages of implementation.

I want to spend a minute discussing a forthcoming Federal action that will have a substantial impact on the States. EPA is preparing a rule directing States to establish carbon dioxide performance standards for existing electricity generation units under Section 111(d) of the Clean Air Act. This rule is understandably controversial but the bottom line is that energy efficiency is the compliance option that can dramatically lower the cost of regulation for both utilities and consumers while achieving substantial carbon dioxide reductions.

States and utilities have a successful track record investing in energy efficiency programs. ESPCs provide an additional opportunity to cost effectively reduce energy demand and deliver carbon dioxide reductions. To date the environmental potential through ESPC projects is far from being captured.

According to a Lawrence Berkeley National Laboratory report, "Barriers to implementing performance contracts remain high in private sector, commercial and industrial facilities," resulting in a penetration rate of less than 10 percent. By allowing States to credit these projects EPA can unlock this potential while also achieving the rulemakings goal of realizing substantial emission reductions at lowest cost.

In closing ESPCs are a valuable, but underutilized private sector financing mechanism that allows governments and building owners to increase their energy efficiency, decrease their energy costs without upfront capital investment. The savings are guaranteed by the contractor.

Chairman Franken and members of this subcommittee, I stand ready to answer any questions you might have.

[The prepared statement of Mr. Clark follows:]

PREPARED STATEMENT OF RANDY CLARK, SENIOR VICE PRESIDENT, NORESCO

Chairman Franken, Ranking Member Risch and members of the subcommittee, thank you for inviting me to testify today regarding private sector mechanisms and financing available to advance energy efficiency in the states.

I am Randy Clark, Senior Vice President, NORESCO, one of the largest energy service companies in the United States utilizing performance-based contracting to deliver energy and maintenance savings and significant infrastructure upgrades to existing facilities. NORESCO is part of UTC Building and Industrial Systems, a unit of United Technologies Corporation. United Technologies is a leading provider to the aerospace and building systems industries employing 220,000 people, including 90,000 in the United States. NORESCO specializes in developing and implementing Energy Savings Performance Contracts for governmental and institutional clients spanning the Federal, state and municipal sectors. In my role at Noresco, I manage the performance contracting business with state agencies, local governments, school districts, public and private universities, and healthcare institutions.

Energy Savings Performance Contracting (ESPCs)

I am here today to discuss how ESPCs deliver energy and cost savings at the state and city level to municipalities, universities, school districts and hospitals (commonly referred to as the "MUSH" market). This same mechanism is also used to deliver cost savings through energy efficiency to multi-family housing agencies. Specifically, I will discuss how this private sector contracting mechanism provides a cost effective pathway toward reducing building energy use, lowering costs and reducing greenhouse gas emissions.

Under an ESPC, a private sector company like Noresco installs new energy efficient equipment at no upfront capital cost to the building owner. ESPCs are typically used for larger facilities or building campuses where there is an opportunity to capture significant energy cost savings. At its most basic, an ESPC converts the money a building owner currently spends on wasted energy into a payment stream that finances energy-saving capital improvements in the facility. The building owner repays this investment over time with funds saved on utility costs. The energy service company will measure, verify and guarantee these energy savings, and private sector financiers provide the capital, which today is available at historically low interest rates. Under the contract, the building owner never pays more than they would have paid for utilities if they had not entered into the ESPC. In addition to generating energy and dollar savings, years of deferred maintenance at buildings are successfully addressed by ESPC projects at no additional cost to the owner. For these reasons, ESPCs have proven to be a highly successful means to implement comprehensive energy efficiency projects.

States are increasingly turning to ESPCs to achieve cost effective energy efficiency. In 2011, Minnesota enacted enabling legislation (16.144/Executive Order 11-12) allowing state agencies to enter into ESPC's. Since that time, the Department of Commerce created the Office of Guaranteed Energy Savings Programs to help pre-qualify Energy Savings Companies (ESCOs) on behalf of state agencies and to provide technical and financial assistance and oversight in the implementation of projects. There are a number of Minnesota state agency projects current under development in this new program.

Over 30 states have now authorized state ESPC programs and the energy service company market is estimated to exceed $5 billion annually. ESPCs provide a number of benefits to the facility, which include:

- Guaranteed performance and cost
- Enhanced reliability and energy security
- Reduced carbon footprint and emissions
- Improved and modernized infrastructure
- Decreased deferred maintenance burden
- Improved indoor working environments

Regional benefits also accrue and include:

- Local job creation of approximately 95 direct and 114 indirect jobs for every $10 million of investment[1]
- Engineering, manufacturing and trade labor engagement
- Small, minority-owned, and women-owned business subcontracting opportunities

Most ESPC contracts range from 12 to 20 years. This allows for the bundling of multiple energy conservation measures; that is, the ability to pull a comprehensive package of energy saving measures together that maximizes energy and cost savings opportunities for the customer. Individual energy conservation measures (ECMs) which can make up a bundled ESPC project may include lighting, building controls, HVAC, boiler or chiller plant improvements, building envelop modifications, water savings, refrigeration, renewable energy systems, load shifting and others. The ESCO guarantees that savings accrue and is reimbursed for their investment over this period.

The market for building energy efficiency projects is strong. According to a 2013 ESCO market survey sponsored by the National Association of Energy Services Companies (NAESCO) and conducted by the Lawrence Berkeley National Laboratory, the total market potential for energy services project investment in non-federal facilities is between $66 and $120 billion. Of that, the investment potential for K12 schools and state and local buildings alone is between $26 and $45 billion. The good

---

[1] Federal Performance Contracting Coalition, accessed February 10, 2014 http://federalperformancecontracting.com/WYSIWYGImage/Job%20Impact%20of%20ESPCs%20chart%20-%20ESPCs.pdf

news is that the ESCO community is capable of delivering these energy savings. According to the 2013 LBNL study, there are more than 140 companies across the U.S. that characterize themselves and serve the marketplace as ESCOs, and 45 of these provide the wide range of supply and demand side services that meet the NAESCO definition of an ESCO

Challenges and Opportunities

Despite the associated benefits of utilizing an ESPC, including financing critical facility improvements without the need for upfront capital, the mechanism is under-utilized. The barriers to increased usage are difficult to quantify but revolve mostly around the fact that performance contracting is different from traditional procurement processes for government and institutions. The vast majority of ESPC projects for MUSH building owners are financed with long-term tax exempt leases or bonds rather than through capital funds or appropriations, but these leases and bonds have their own challenges especially in light of the increased uncertainty around state and local tax revenues since the economic downturn in late 2008. Overall, MUSH building owners have been reluctant to incur new or additional debt related to building improvements even when the building improvements are 100 percent funded from energy and operational savings.

According to a 2008 LBNL study, the differences in the penetration rates of ESPC projects in the surveyed states appear to be related to the ability of state governments to overcome policy and programmatic barriers to ESPC implementation. The study included among its recommendations that State agencies should consider pursuing funding and technical assistance available through ratepayer-funded energy efficiency programs administered by utilities or third party administrators, and possibly integrating these resources with ESCO-delivered energy efficiency investments to maximize the level of dollar and energy savings to be mined from state facilities.

Some states are taking steps to address these barriers. The State of Delaware created the Sustainable Energy Utility (SEU) to assist with and encourage energy performance contracting for buildings in the State. The SEU issues tax-exempt debt on behalf of public entities in the State in order to fund the investment in building infrastructure. The SEU issued $70 million of bonds in late 2011 and has a number of comprehensive energy efficiency projects completed or in the final stages of implementation. The Maryland Clean Energy Center is pursuing a similar approach to facilitating the financing of energy efficiency projects as is the Chicago Infrastructure Trust. In Massachusetts, a project recently completed by NORESCO with the University of Massachusetts Dartmouth was supported by $2.7 million of investment from the local utility, NSTAR. This project is expected to reduce greenhouse gas emissions by 16,000 tons (CO_2 equivalent).

ESPCs Provide an Opportunity to Cost Effectively Lower Greenhouse Gas Emissions

The Environmental Protection Agency (EPA) is preparing to propose a rule directing states to establish carbon dioxide performance standards for existing electricity generation units under Section 111(d) of the Clean Air Act. This rule is understandably controversial and there are many perspectives about how EPA might best enable State flexibility in giving utilities a menu of cost effective compliance options. The fact of the matter is that when this rule is finalized, energy efficiency is the compliance option that can dramatically lower the cost of regulation for both utilities and consumers while achieving substantial carbon dioxide reductions.

States and utilities have a long, successful track record in investing in energy efficiency programs. These programs include demand response initiatives, energy efficient appliance rebate programs and education efforts. ESPCs provide an additional and largely unrealized opportunity to cost effectively reduce energy demand and deliver carbon dioxide reductions. In addition, energy service companies are already responsible for measuring, verifying and sustaining the energy savings over long periods of time, so the emission reductions are real.

To date, the environmental potential through ESPC projects is far from being fully realized. According to a Lawrence Berkeley National Laboratory report, "barriers to implementing performance contracts remain high enough in private sector commercial and industrial facilities," resulting in a penetration rate of less than 10 percent. By allowing states to satisfy reduction goals under such carbon dioxide performance standards through ESPC projects, EPA can unlock this potential while also achieving the rulemaking's goal of realizing substantial emission reductions at lowest cost.

The mechanism for crediting major building energy efficiency investments under a Section 111(d) compliance plan can build on widely accepted approaches already implemented in the private sector for major energy efficiency projects. Therefore, EPA should (1) recognize ESPC projects as a favored method towards meeting compliance; (2) require States to include measurement, monitoring, verification and reporting results for all contractual methods of energy efficiency used to meet the EPA compliance requirement; and (3) provide additional procedures needed to translate energy savings into creditable emission reductions.

Conclusion

In summary, ESPCs are a private sector financing mechanism that allows governments and building owners to increase their energy efficiency, decrease their energy costs without upfront investment and the savings are guaranteed by the contractor.

Chairman Franken and members of this subcommittee, thank you for the opportunity to appear before you today. I stand ready to answer any questions you might have.

Senator FRANKEN. Thank you, Mr. Clark.

That is, what you're talking about is providing flexibilities for States to do energy efficiency offsets for these new rules on existing coal fired plants, etcetera. So and I think that's very, very interesting.

Finally, Mr. Rodgers.

STATEMENT OF WILLIAM A. RODGERS, JR., CHIEF EXECUTIVE OFFICER AND PRESIDENT, GOODCENTS HOLDINGS, INC., ATLANTA, GA

Mr. RODGERS. Right.

Chairman Franken, Ranking Member Risch, Senator Portman, my name is Bill Rodgers and I am the President and CEO of GoodCents Holdings which is headquartered in Atlanta, Georgia. We provide operations in 22 States as well as Canada and we deliver over 85 energy efficiency programs currently.

I thank you for the opportunity to testify before you today on the important topic of energy efficiency and the lessons learned from State programs.

Two years ago I was privileged to testify before this committee on an innovative concept using an energy efficiency program to supplement new generation capability. The State of Indiana, recognizing the need to balance clean air considerations with reliable and affordable electricity chartered a middle course by enacting long term energy efficiency standards. At that time this program was in its infancy and now today, it has matured into a broad based energy efficiency program covering a full spectrum of services.

From the initial program design focused on delivery of targeted savings to the critical marketing services which derive customer education and behavior, to the field implementation and last the measurement and verification of the program's actual savings. This program provides a template for other States grappling with similar concerns and should serve as an example for this committee of the type of results can be achieved when regulators, power companies, consumers and environmental groups all work together toward a common goal.

Let me explain how we've done this.

In 2009 the State of Indiana took a firm stance on energy conservation and established an aggressive time line to achieve annual savings goals over a 10-year period. Through a coordination committee of the Utility Regulatory Commission, made up of representatives of each of the utilities, municipalities and consumer groups in the State, they went to the marketplace and selected our company, GoodCents as the independent third party administrator for this statewide initiative. Branded Energizing Indiana, the initiative is a united effort by the State participating utilities, businesses, residents and consumer organizations to offer energy efficiency programs that will benefit communities all across the State.

This extensive statewide suite of 6 core energy efficiency programs includes commercial and industrial customer projects, residential/home energy assessments, income qualified weatherization program, residential lighting expansion through participating retail locations and energy educational programs and building assessments for Indiana schools. As Administrator, GoodCents coordinates, manages, implements and reports on this core suite of programs to meet the annual energy savings goals identified for each participating utility.

A few accomplishments over the past 2 years, if I may share with you.

First and foremost we created nearly 400 new jobs in the State of Indiana.

We've enrolled over 200,000 residential customers into these programs.

We've worked with almost a thousand retail stores to sell an excess of 6 million energy efficient light bulbs.

We've educated over 155,000 elementary school students about energy efficiency.

We've established a network of over 2,000 nonprofit organizations representing over a million members to educate and market the programs.

We've developed a statewide trade ally network that has delivered over $450 million in energy savings projects to the commercial and industrial sector.

Most importantly, we've achieved over 900 million kilowatt hours of energy savings which is enough to power the residents of Boise, Idaho for an entire year.

GoodCents strongly believes that by consolidating energy efficiency programs into one core initiative Energizing Indiana has benefited many utility customers including the businesses, schools and homeowners. The power of offering an integrated and tailored approach most definitely drives increased productivity, consistent branding and marketing messages and ultimately the highest value, most cost effective program for its customers.

Similar to the driving force behind Indiana many other States have established their own standards. Once these have been set they develop the proper alignment between all stakeholders to drive toward their aggressive goals. This allows for the best thinking to be put toward the market based program requirements verses establishing Federal prescriptive programs that become difficult to realize ultimate success.

Costs of these programs are market driven and tested as well as included into the local rate structures. The market forces ultimately drive participation and returns once the standards are established. These structures allow for a uniform measurement system affording the required transparency of the return on investment and energy impact.

Two years ago the debate in Washington was how to best incentivize and grow efficiency programs and what, if any impact, would they have on energy use? Today we know that these programs not only can thrive, independent of Federal subsidies and support, but also that their results can be measured, can be verified and that efficiency can deliver savings to rate payers and utilities alike.

We must continue to build on this progress. As Congress and the Administration look to balance the seemingly competing need for abundant, affordable energy with environmental considerations, energy efficiency programs can and must be part of the overall systems based solution.

I thank you for the opportunity to be here with you today and look forward to any questions you may have.

[The prepared statement of Mr. Rodgers follows:]

PREPARED STATEMENT OF WILLIAM A. RODGERS, JR., CHIEF EXECUTIVE OFFICER AND PRESIDENT, GOODCENTS HOLDINGS, INC., ATLANTA, GA

GoodCents Overview

Mr. Chairman and members of the Committee on Energy and Natural Resources, my name is Bill Rodgers and I am the President and CEO of GoodCents Holdings, Inc. GoodCents is headquartered in Atlanta, Georgia and provides operations in 22 states as well as Canada delivering over 85 energy efficiency programs. I thank you for the opportunity to testify before you today on the important topic of energy efficiency. Our company has been in existence for over 34 years and has provided multiple types of Demand Side Management and Energy Efficiency programs to over 150 Utilities, including Investor-Owned, Co-operatives and Municipalities. We have over 600 employees located across North America who wake up each and every morning focused on helping both residents and businesses learn to utilize their energy in a more efficient and smarter fashion, as well as conserving as much energy as possible.

Our company partners with both electric and gas Utilities to deliver the most effective programs targeted at reducing their energy footprint. Some of the programs we deliver are:

- Facility Audits (both residential and commercial)
- Income Qualified Weatherization
- Residential and Commercial Rebate Programs
  —Trade Ally Network development and management
- Equipment Efficiency Studies
- Retrofit Programs for Commercial and Industrial
  —Lighting
  —H.V.A.C.
- Equipment (motors, drives, refrigeration etc.)Energy End-Use Studies Our involvement covers the full spectrum of services: From initial program design, focused on the delivery of required or targeted savings; to the critical marketing services which drive customer education and program enrollments; to field implementation; and lastly, the measurement and verification of the program's actual savings which are reported back to the respective regulatory body. Since the purpose of this hearing is to consider lessons learned from state efficiency and renewable programs, I would like to call your attention to the Energizing Indiana program. GoodCents has lead as the Third Party Administrator of this state-wide, multiple-utility program since 2011.

Energizing Indiana Overview

In 2009, the State of Indiana joined many other states, and since that time many others have followed, to establish long-term Energy Efficiency Resource Standards (EERS). These standards set forth energy savings targets with specific timetables for achievement. Once the EERS were established, Indiana undertook an exhaustive review of their options for goal achievement. Their model evaluated the need for a true partnership of all stakeholders in order to achieve their goals. They established a Demand Side Management Coordination Committee (DSMCC) of the Indiana Utility Regulatory Commission (IURC) made up of representatives of each of the Utilities, municipalities and consumer groups in the state. They went to the marketplace to select an Independent Third Party Administrator for their statewide initiative. GoodCents was selected and entered into a contract targeted at aggressive energy savings over the first two contract years of 2012 and 2013. Branded "Energizing Indiana," the initiative is a united effort by the state, participating Utilities, businesses, residents, and consumer organizations to offer energy efficiency programs that will benefit communities across the state.

This extensive, state-wide suite of six core energy efficiency programs includes: Commercial & Industrial Prescriptive program targeting the most energy consuming equipment and process improvements, Residential Home Energy Assessments, Income-Qualified Weatherization Services, Residential Lighting expansion through participating retail locations, Energy Educational Programs and Commercial Building Assessments for Indiana Schools.

As administrator, GoodCents coordinates, manages, implements and reports on this core suite of programs to meet the annual energy savings goals identified for each participating Utility. A few key and central accomplishments over the past two years:

- Created nearly 400 new Indiana jobs
- Enrolled over 200,000 residential customers
- Worked with 960 retail stores to sell over 6,200,000 energy efficient bulbs
- Educated over 155,000 elementary students about energy efficiency within their own homes
- Established a network of over 2,000 non-profit organizations representing over 1,000,000 members to educate and market the programs
- Energy Advisors logged over 4,600,000 miles serving the residents and businesses throughout Indiana
- Installed over 800,000 measures in commercial and industrial facilities
- Achieved over 900,000,000 kWh of energy savings in just the first two years which is enough to power the residents of Salt Lake City, Utah for an entire year.

In addition, the Utilities also offer other "Core Plus" programs directed toward expanding to an even greater suite of energy efficiency services that GoodCents works to educate the ultimate customers on the combined value. GoodCents has built a world-class team of experienced professionals from across the state of Indiana and is managing the program from offices in Indianapolis, Crown Point, Fort Wayne, and Evansville.

GoodCents strongly believes that by consolidating energy efficiency programs into one core initiative, Energizing Indiana has benefitted many Utility customers, including industry, businesses, schools, and homeowners. The power of offering an integrated and tailored approach most definitely drives increased productivity, consistent branding and marketing messages, and ultimately the highest value, most cost-effective programs for customers.

Driving Program Success

Through our years of experience implementing energy efficiency programs like Energizing Indiana we have found that program success is driven primarily by two factors:

- Is the program designed to achieve savings; and
- Is it effectively implemented and marketed to reach out to customers to engage, educate and ultimately drive participation.

Below is a further overview of the Demand Response and Energy Efficiency programs currently being successfully delivered by GoodCents through our design, marketing and implementation efforts.

Demand Response Programs

For more than three decades, GoodCents has been a valued partner for Utilities implementing and leveraging home area networking, advanced metering infrastructure and demand response programs.

GoodCents combines smart meter deployment, infrastructure component installation, proprietary scheduling and routing applications, and customer call to ensure the most efficient and successful deployment of smart grid programs.

We utilize decades of experience in implementing and installing demand response program equipment such as communicating thermostats, water heaters and pool pumps. We also work inside the home to leverage the optimal solutions for our customers in establishing the most effective home area networks to allow for maximum understanding of customers home energy usage. Home area networks connect all aspects of the home to best understand how, where and to what degree energy is being used.

GoodCents' demand response portfolio includes programs in California, Georgia, Illinois, Indiana, Utah, North Carolina, Ohio, South Carolina, Virginia, Nevada, Kentucky, Oklahoma and Washington.

Energy Efficiency Programs

The goals of the energy efficiency programs offered by GoodCents are to provide Utilities and their customers, both residential and commercial, with an avenue to reduce energy and demand requirements, save money on electric bills, and meet energy reduction goals set forth by state legislatures and commissions. The three most popular residential programs to be utilized are Income-Qualified

Weatherization, Rebates, and Home Energy Assessments. In order to impact usage on a larger scale, commercial programs such as Commercial/Industrial Energy Assessments, and Custom and Prescriptive Rebates must be leveraged.

Residential Energy Efficiency

GoodCents believes that on-site energy assessments provide the best opportunity to reshape the energy usage habits of all customers, for both Income-Qualified Weatherization and Home Energy Assessment programs. Our highly trained and experienced advisors perform detailed site surveys and work closely with the customer to install energy efficiency measures as determined by the Utility and their customers. Our program delivery may include combustion safety testing, blower door guided air sealing, arranging for improved attic insulation, providing conservation education, and encouraging adoption of energy efficiency measures.

Along with installing measures, we are also capable and equipped to conduct in-out testing for implementation-style assessments such as weatherization, duct repairs, ceiling insulation and more. We are then able to educate the homeowner on the most impactful improvements they can make to their home to increase efficiency. Typically these improvements are supported through utility-funded Rebate programs. GoodCents generally uses six common elements for on-site energy efficiency programs: pre-visit and authorization, home health and safety, installed measures, energy audit inputs, energy audit analytic engine, and homeowner's energy report. Our portfolio includes program implementations in Indiana, Ohio, West Virginia, Florida, Virginia, Kentucky North and South Carolina.

Commercial & Industrial Energy Assessments

GoodCents' Commercial and Industrial programs include energy assessments that are supported by prescriptive and custom incentive structures that reward participants with monetary incentives based on installation of energy efficiency equipment upgrades. Following the energy assessment, the customer is educated on the most cost effective improvements to implement at their business that will reduce the greatest amount of energy. These upgrades include lighting, motors and pumps, HVAC, and potentially other equipment such as ENERGY STARr transformers and efficient package refrigeration. Incentives are provided for one-for-one replacements, retrofits and new installations of qualified equipment.

The objectives of the C&I Prescriptive Program are to:

- Lower electric energy consumption in the C&I market sector.
- Help C&I customers decrease their overall energy costs.
- Build market-based activity that captures near and long-term energy and demand savings.
- Encourage equipment vendors and contractors to actively promote and install energy efficient technologies for their C&I customers.

Active Programs are being delivered in Indiana, Kentucky, North Carolina, Ohio, South Carolina, Virginia and West Virginia.

Customer Engagement and Participation

Through years of experience, GoodCents has identified a variety of tools that are effective in engaging customers and changing their behavior, resulting in optimal program enrollment. The key to a program's success is establishing a strong marketing campaign that spans multiple channels and provides multiple touches to Utility customers to increase both awareness and program participation. In addition, it is essential to develop an enrollment channel that is easy and convenient for customers to use.

Effective marketing is the key to robust participation. GoodCents has a complete array of marketing capabilities including print collateral design and production, social marketing programs (community engagement programs, social media implementation, local enrichment programs, etc.), and electronic communications to include website development, landing pages, email campaigns, and online program administration. In many programs, incentives are used to drive higher response rates through direct mail, trade ally networks, and community enrichment.

GoodCents also works with Utilities to establish program awareness through social marketing platforms and pushes to engage local newspapers and media channels for additional support. In addition, we leverage social media resources such as Facebook, Twitter, and YouTube to raise awareness of energy efficiency and demand response programs. GoodCents works with the Utility to build a program webpage that provides program information and allows the customers to enroll. In addition, we leverage some program marketing approaches with many of the Utility's current and future media campaigns or marketing efforts.

When working within the energy efficiency business the key to gaining both commercial and residential customer acceptance is in educating them as to the benefits of the programs, allowing them to understand the financial impact and return on their investment, and working to make the participation process simple. Page 14 of 14

Conclusion

Similar to the driving force behind Energizing Indiana, many other states have established their own Energy Efficiency Resource Standards. Once these goals and standards have been set they then develop the proper alignment between the state, regulators, local communities, Utilities, industrial and commercial businesses and residential customers to drive towards their aggressive goals. This allows for the best thinking to be put towards the market-based program requirements versus establishing federal prescriptive programs that become difficult to realize ultimate success. Costs of these programs are market driven and tested as well as the proper review and inclusion in the local rate structures. The market forces ultimately drive the programs, participation and returns once the standards are established. These structures allow for a standard and common measurement system that drives the most consistent and clear understanding of the return on investment and energy impact.

Senator FRANKEN. Thank you, Mr. Rodgers.

I'm going to go to Senator Portman, but just I love the idea of energy efficiency education for kids. I've often thought that we should—I'm on the Education Committee, that we should reinvent, we should re-establish Home Ec and that home economics should include financial literacy. It should include nutrition, about how to cook nutritiously and I think it should involve how to keep your home energy efficient.

Let's go to Senator Portman.

Senator PORTMAN. Thank you. Thank you, Mr. Chairman for having this hearing and for the great testimony that you've brought before us. I'm really impressed with what you have going on in your States and some of the examples we've heard from today.

As you know this Portman/Shaheen bill that the chairman called it, is really called Shaheen/Portman, but she's not here. So we're going to change the name for this purpose.

But Jeanne did testify earlier, I understand, correct?

Senator FRANKEN. She did. It was Shaheen/Portman then.

Senator PORTMAN. Yes. That doesn't surprise me.

[Laughter.]

Senator PORTMAN. She's no longer on the committee so we can get away with this now and again.

But we are hoping to get it up soon. Thank you for all the help many of you have provided. I know there have been some disappointments we haven't been able to do more in this first piece of legislation. But it is really a huge step forward.

I take the position that we should have an all of the above strategy. I think that includes natural gas production in States like Ohio, but also energy efficiency, certainly renewables, coal in Ohio, oil, nuclear. Our legislation is consistent with what you talked about today in the sense that as was just stated, I think, well by Mr. Rodgers, you know, it doesn't have mandates.

It does have incentives. It does rely on the market. It does have some new provisions and new office funding. I think it's the kind of thing that will have a very substantial impact on efficiency but without losing the bipartisan support that it's had thus far. So that's our hope. I'm hopeful we'll see something even in the next month on it on the Floor of the Senate.

We think now on the bill that will be reintroduced probably not next week because we're out of session, but the next week we'll have a deficit reduction component as well of about $10 million. We'll also have a lot more savings than that because it requires the Federal Government, the largest user of energy in the world, to be more efficient and that will save taxpayers a lot in the long run. So I think we can argue this is also cost effective.

It does have some good support including the Chamber of Commerce, National Association of Manufacturers, the Environmental Defense Fund, American Chemistry Council, Alliance to Save Energy, among others. Significantly distinguished groups represented here today. Like NASEO the ACEEE, thank you, and NORESCO have all been great and supportive and we appreciate that, again, even when sometimes you haven't gotten everything in that you wanted.

Thanks to the work of Chairman Wyden and Ranking Member Murkowski we now have 10 additional bipartisan provisions we're adding to the bill to improve energy efficiency to the Federal Government, to deal with some of the regulatory barriers to private companies looking to save energy. These provisions have allowed us to pick up the support now of the American Gas Association, the Edison Electric Institute, the National Rural Electric Cooperative Association and others. We have about 270 groups so far.

One of those amendments is authored by your own Senator, Mr. Franken, who happens to be here today. I would have mentioned it anyway even if he wasn't.

Another one of the amendments is actually, Mr. Risch, who just left us. I know his staff is still here so they will like the fact that I'm calling it Risch/Udall rather than Udall/Risch.

We thank Senator Franken.

Senator FRANKEN. I sense a pattern.

Senator PORTMAN. Yes.

But it's good stuff. It got through this committee with a 19 to 3 vote which is unusual. Now again, we're working to try to re-introduce this bill with a lot more amendments included in the bill, the base bill, and frankly, therefore some more support and some more substance in the legislation.

I've got 3 quick questions.

One is for Mr. Rodgers. On your testimony you talked a lot about efficiency being best tailored, specifically, to State requirements, conditions driven by markets. From your experience if a consumer is able to receive a clear picture of what the benefits are of a particular energy efficiency investment are they likely to make a reasonable decision on their own that reduces energy costs and saves them money?

Mr. RODGERS. Thank you, Senator.

I think that's probably one of the biggest challenges our industry has always faced. That's one of an educational component ensuring that the customers truly understand how and when energy is being utilized. We have found that when that education is put into place and in many cases it's now being put in place through technology, they absolutely will behave and take the steps necessary on their own to participate in energy saving measures.

It is typically when they are not as aware. I always like to use the story of if we all when we go to the grocery store only got a bill from the grocery store at the end of the month we would have no idea how to best curb the spending there. The same thing happens now with the utility bill. We don't have the insight and the knowledge. But that technology is continuing to be spread across the country which I think is driving that proper behavior.

Senator PORTMAN. I appreciate that experience you bring at the end of the day when of the business that you're in. I agree with you entirely. Of course, we do have some new amendments in the bill along those lines. Bennet and Ayotte establishing a voluntary certification recognition program to promote efficiency in commercial buildings.

Senators Isakson and Bennet, as you may know, we have that legislation now as part of ours which it's going to be quite substantial in its effect, I believe, aimed at encouraging residential efficiency investments by allowing the homes expected energy cost savings to be factored into its value and affordability, part of the mortgage process.

Then finally, Senator Franken's bill which requires federally leased buildings to benchmark energy usage data.

Those are all, again, included now in the base legislation which I think will make consistent with what you're talking about.

To Mr. Taylor, thank you again to you and NASEO for your continued support. I know some of the provisions, again, fell out of the bill that you had hoped would be part of it. We just appreciate the support of the organization. We want to continue to work with you on that.

Mr. Nadel, so many questions but if you can tell us just briefly what you have learned in your economic analysis of Shaheen/Portman. Maybe you could speak a little bit to some of the benefits that you have measured quickly and what kind of energy savings we can expect if the bill is enacted into law?

Mr. NADEL. OK, certainly.

Senator PORTMAN. I thought you'd be ready for that. I'd thought you'd have your paper.

Mr. NADEL. Oh, OK.

Senator Shaheen actually summarized the benefits from our recent analysis. I did not bring those with you. But they are very substantial in terms of large energy savings many, you know, more than a hundred thousand jobs.

I'd be happy to supply those for the record. I didn't bring them with me.

Senator PORTMAN. That would be great.

Senator PORTMAN. By 2030 energy savings that equal 12 quads, the equivalent of taking roughly 80 million homes off the grid, a cumulative savings amount to $100 billion by 2030. As you say, there's also some jobs figures you were able to provide us with which we really appreciate. I think it was 130 thousand, if I'm not mistaken.

So thank you.

Maybe for the record, Mr. Chairman, if we could that, that would be great.

Again, thank you all very much for being here today. To the Chairman, thank you for your indulgence. We really look forward to working with all of you to try to move this legislation forward.

Again, I think even within the next month we have a good opportunity.

Thank you very much.

Senator FRANKEN. Thank you, Senator, for your great work in Shaheen/Portman.

I guess I've got you all to myself so since I do—and by the way Senator Risch's questions will be submitted for the record. OK?

Senator FRANKEN. I do want to talk a little bit about propane right at the start. This is on energy efficiency and renewables, but I just want to talk a little bit about that.

We had kind of a perfect storm and we saw the price of propane go from under $2 to over $6. Commissioner Rothman and I met with some folks at a farm near Faribault, Minnesota this weekend. It seems that it is the crisis is the worst, seems to be, over hopefully. But we are going to in 8 months be back to the drawing season for our corn and our grain and then we'll have another winter.

So, we saw some good things happening, including since we have a representative from Texas here, that we saw some propane coming up on the pipeline. We saw some trucked up. I just want to ask our Minnesota and Texas representatives here what your thoughts are on going forward how we can ensure faster delivery of propane on pipelines, on rails and on other modes, like trucking during emergencies.

Any thoughts.

Yes, Mr. Rothman.

Mr. ROTHMAN. Mr. Chair, thank you.

The one thing I would like to note, at least for Minnesota is that, as you know, the Cochin pipeline coming down from Canada is scheduled to reverse flow. So if——

Senator FRANKEN. That's 40 percent of our propane comes from that pipeline. It's reversing for next year, right?

Mr. ROTHMAN. Exactly.

So in addition to the weather and the crop issues we have a delivery/pipeline problem. We've urged and I think with your leadership urging all of the pipelines, the marketers, the suppliers, distributors from the reserves that we have, the supplies that we have throughout the United States to the home in Minnesota needs to be examined very carefully.

Senator FRANKEN. We will do that either in the subcommittee or as the committee as a whole we need to be looking at this in anticipation of next year.

Mr. ROTHMAN. That's great.

In addition it is part of the things—and Mr. Chair, maybe what I'd like to do is just suggest. We were collecting in the Administration, some ideas and suggestions for legislation, perhaps either for you, things at the State level and then things that we see as necessary. You know, off the top, there's potential for looking at a propane reserve system for the Midwest, just for crisis situation.

I bumped into a friend over the weekend who said he had recently switched off of propane to natural gas for the home but used the Federal tax credit as financing to help do that. I don't know if that's still in place or not or whatever.

What I would say is that we'll submit and work with you to develop, you know, good alternatives to solve a problem or at least mitigate the problem as it goes into next winter and appreciate that opportunity.

Senator FRANKEN. Mr. Taylor, any thoughts? Just I know this isn't necessarily your area in Texas, but.

Mr. TAYLOR. Thank you, yes.

From a supply perspective propane, of course, is the byproduct of natural gas processing and petroleum refining. So where those activities occur you tend to have supplies of propane stored in large volumes. In Texas, Mont Belleview is the largest storage area and the pricing basis point for wholesale supply.

The challenge with propane is getting it, is moving it from those large stores to places where it's consumed. The recent FERC action allowing propane to flow north on a priority basis certainly helps. But that still takes, in some cases, weeks for that product to move through the pipeline.

Senator FRANKEN. Right.

Mr. TAYLOR. The starting process is like that earlier. It's certainly important. As a backstop of sorts, moving propane by rail, although rail lines are congested with other traffic, but by truck is another alternative in moving smaller shipments.

In our State our Governor initiated a waiver and renewed that recently allowing out of State trucks and drivers to come into Texas, come to propane terminals, fill their trucks and move back north and into the Midwest. So that's certainly an action that is allowable under our State law and I assume will continue on.

Senator FRANKEN. The Department of Transportation did a waiver on ours as a service for truck drivers. So, but that can only last so long.

[Laughter.]

Senator FRANKEN. Before you get a different kind of problem.

I like the idea of a propane reserve system for the Midwest. It could be similar to a model that already exists for heating oil reserve in the Northeast. So we'll look into that.

Let's segway from heating, keeping people warm in the winter to some—to this what we're talking about here which is weatherization, the Weatherization Assistance Program.

This is Mr. Rodgers, Mr. Nadel or any other panelist. What can we do at the Federal level to incentivize or to help do weatherization?

Mr. Nadel.

Mr. NADEL. I can take a stab a little bit at it.

I think helping to provide good financing for consumers to help finance weatherization would be very useful. I would particularly note the on bill financing that Hawaii has as well as New York, California is starting it. This allows consumers to basically get the money through the utility bill, sometimes from the utility, sometimes through a third party financer who works with the utility and then they make the payment on the bill. So it makes it very easy.

The Federal Government can provide technical assistance and help facilitate it. I'm not saying that they'd provide the capital, but that would be very useful.

As Senator Portman said, more education on what people can do, more technical assistance working through the States would be very helpful as well, obviously if we're talking low income weatherization funding for the Weatherization Assistance Program.

Then I'd point out whatever can be done to encourage utility sector and energy efficiency programs because the utilities are often helping to provide technical assistance and other support for weatherization would be very useful.

A final comment I would make is while the utilities are very helpful if we're talking things like propane or oil you need these other measures to help it. The utilities are great for natural gas and for electricity, but I think all too often propane and fuel oil efficiency has not gotten the attention it needs. The crisis helps point to the need for that. If we can reduce the demand, obviously we're not going to do it this winter, but gradually weatherize these homes.

I've heard reports. We have one person in our office whose uncle lives in Minnesota and he's getting like a $10,000 propane bill this year for not a very large farmhouse. I'm sure you've heard many more. But how do we make those homes more——

Senator FRANKEN. All of our buildings more efficient is one of the things that we're talking about. You're talking about financing models. I just, but I know Mr. Rodgers has something to say.

But I do want to ask about—it seems that this comes up a lot whether we're talking about energy savings, performance contracts or whether we're talking about pace. We talk a lot about financing mechanisms, but Mr. Rodgers, what were you going to say?

Mr. RODGERS. Mr. Chairman, I think the—what I would add to what has already been said is we manage literally thousands of weatherization projects a year across the country. These are all through the utilities, who I think the utilities do a tremendous job in being able to support their customers and driving these very important programs.

But I think I'll play off a little bit of question that Senator Portman had asked earlier and that's in the area of education. I think that's one thing that all customers need to have more of and that is an understanding of how energy is being used within their home and what are the things that they can do to help prevent rising costs to help prevent leaking/leakage out of their homes.

We find, when we go into income qualified communities and work with the residents they are incredibly supportive and embracing of all of the activities that the utilities are providing as long as they understand what the impact is going to be on their home.

So, I think if we think about it both at the Federal level and at the State level an increase in education, an increase in knowledge, for these end customers to really be able to understand what these various measures will do for their home, I think is a critically, critically, important element.

Senator FRANKEN. Mr. Nadel was talking about getting help from utilities to do these things. In Minnesota we have an energy efficiency standard. Now it's called—you talk about having standards, but not mandates, right? That was part of your testimony.

What's the difference really? I mean, if you're saying to the utilities this is—you have to improve your customer's energy efficiency by 1.5 percent every year. That's a mandate, isn't it? That standard is a mandate.

That incentivizes utilities to help finance weatherization. Doesn't it?

I mean is there something that we're being a little too cute when we talk about the difference between saying we need standards, but not mandates. Aren't mandates useful?

Anyone want to take that or Mr. Rodgers, I seem to be talking to your——

Mr. RODGERS. Mr. Chairman, I think when you break down the difference in my mind. The standards are setting, you know, kind of the goals and objectives as to what you want to accomplish within that State. The mandates, as I think about mandates, start to become more prescriptive as far as how you go about doing that.

So if we think of those as really higher level goals and objectives to allow the market and the utilities within those markets to really, you know, reach out and bring the best of what companies like ours have to bear to their customers, you know, I think they can be viewed as one and the same.

I think my concern when I talk about mandates are really starting to see that those prescriptive requirements are coming at a higher level where really we need to allow the market to drive what those prescriptive measures would be.

Senator FRANKEN. Right.

You can voluntary standards or mandatory standards, but in, I think, that in many cases we're talking about a distinction without a difference that a standard is a mandate.

Mr. RODGERS. Right.

Senator FRANKEN. But it's a mandate that's not so prescriptive that it allows the market to figure out how to meet that standard.

Commissioner Rothman.

Mr. ROTHMAN. Mr. Chair, to your point.

I think all stakeholders have an opportunity. Utilities, consumers, everybody, the environmental community to focus on the fact that you can achieve through a standard certainty, certainty not just having a goal, but in achieving something which results in carbon reduction and efficiency standards. But also creates the certainty from the public policy perspective that's necessary to lay the foundation so that utilities can work with something and understand what that policy is. With that certainty you get a better business outcome for them and for the States by having the standard.

So as to whether it's useful, it's absolutely helpful.

Senator FRANKEN. We have an energy efficiency standard or I'm sorry, a renewable portfolio standard in Minnesota of 25 percent by 2025 for Xcel it's 30 by 20, right?

Mr. ROTHMAN. Yes.

Senator FRANKEN. Then we're meeting that, as you said.

Mr. ROTHMAN. Yes.

Senator FRANKEN. Mr. Nadel, can you give us a broad overview of how these programs and they are mandates, how they're working across the country that the States have decided to impose upon themselves through their legislature or through their Governors?

Mr. NADEL. Yes. At this point 26 States have established energy saving goals that kind of have mandatory nature to them, meaning there are rewards for hitting them or perhaps some consequences for not. They set these standards based on past experience, based on neighboring States, based on studies what is cost effective. Nobody sets a standard being a pie in the sky. They set them based on what they can achieve.

We're in the process of coming out with a report probably next month on the results of these States and how well they're doing. Updating a report we did a couple of years ago. What we're finding is the vast majority of States are either exceeding their standards, equaling them or coming very close. Only in a few cases are they falling a little bit short.

But when they have these levels they really sharpen their pencils and figure out how to do them. They are very flexible. So typically, now in Minnesota it's one and a half percent savings a year. It doesn't say how much comes from weatherization verses commercial lighting etcetera. The utilities have a lot of flexibility to do them.

As someone who used to work in the utility industry and has a lot of friends there, I have noticed that these people really pay attention to hitting their goals. I had I remember one friend telling me that whenever he bumped into the CEO of his company, the guy would always ask him, so how are you coming on your goals because in that case one, they cared, but 2, they actually stood to make more than a million dollars in extra shareholder incentives from hitting their goals. We now have over 20 States that have type of incentive.

So I think they can work very well. But they do have a lot of flexibility to, you know, they're not highly prescriptive. It's achieve these savings the best way you can.

Senator FRANKEN. Which is what Mr. Rodgers was saying that they're flexible not overly prescriptive, but they're all learning from each other.

Mr. Glick, Mr. Rothman, Mr. Taylor, do you want to talk about how your—what your successes and challenges in implementing your standards have been in your States?

Mr. GLICK. Sure, Chairman Franken.

In Hawaii what we've noticed is that success has come—has raised a lot of challenges. So we have now a number of circuits which were overloaded. Hawaiian Electric estimates that 20 or 30 percent of circuits on Oahu, our population center, are overloaded.

So most of our work today is how do we solve those problems? How do we work to create better renewable penetration?

So a lot of our solutions now are looking to short term efforts, the things that we can use in the SEP or State energy program.

Senator FRANKEN. When you mean overloaded you mean your base load doesn't meet high demand, peak hours or something? Is that what you're saying?

Mr. GLICK. Yes, what I'm——

Senator FRANKEN. OK, I just wanted to make sure I understood.

Mr. GLICK. Sure. It means that at certain times of the day we may be exceeding peak penetration levels by, you know, we may have 120 percent of our capacity. It's overloaded. That means we curtail renewable energy because we have too much producing at that time.

We also have reduced demand because of our energy portfolio standard and because of conservation efforts. So it's a matter of balance.

Senator FRANKEN. Oh, I'm sorry. Your output is exceeding your need.

Mr. GLICK. That's right.

Senator FRANKEN. Oh, I see what you're saying.

Now are you doing any kinds of things like storage in order to deal with that?

Mr. GLICK. Immediately there are smart inverters that can help ease some of the burden. Another technical fixes that can happen, either the residential or the utility level, but the medium term fixes include a lot of energy storage, pump storage strategies that are being pursued in Kauai, Maui, on Oahu.

Long term combining our grids because we are unique in the sense that we have 6 independent grids. Just the combination of unifying the Maui and Oahu grids could increase overall penetration by another 53 megawatts because of the redundancy in the system that it will eliminate.

Senator FRANKEN. That's laying a cable.

Mr. GLICK. It's an undersea cable.

Senator FRANKEN. On the ocean floor or?

Mr. GLICK. Basically, yeah, that's right which have been done throughout the world.

Senator FRANKEN. Right.

Mr. GLICK. There's over 50 instances of successful undersea cables.

Senator FRANKEN. OK.

Either Commissioner Rothman or Director Taylor?

Mr. ROTHMAN. Chairman, let me address the 3 various standards that we have quickly.

On the Conservation Improvement Program, you know, as Mr. Nadel said and suggested, Minnesota has all the utilities file and, you know, plans for their CIP. Working with them there's a really good dialog. It's a great opportunity.

Over time many of the low hanging fruit projects, obviously, have been taken into account. Continuing those successes are important.

On the RES, the Renewable Energy Standard, I'd say the challenge is making sure we have the infrastructure in place, the grid technology, to keep unlocking our renewable energy in our sector, in Minnesota, as you know.

Then in the new solar one, I think it's going to be finding the best, appropriate solar strategies to meet those challenges and how the market will play out over the next 5/10 years where we have a bunch of strategies in place and hopefully we'll take some lessons from Hawaii and achieve our goals there.

Mr. TAYLOR. Mr. Chairman, in Texas in 1999 we passed legislation to restructure our electric markets. We have competitive retail markets. In the place of what had been utility efficiency programs under a regulated, fully integrated, investor owned utility model, those transferred over to what we know as the Energy Efficiency Portfolio Standard. I think it may have been one of the first, if not the first, in the country.

The first, OK.

[Laughter.]

Mr. TAYLOR. Originally that started off as a 10-percent offset in growth and demand for electricity customers within the investor owned service areas. That has now grown to 20 and now 30 percent offset. The utilities have exceeded that goal in each of the past several years.

A few years ago a performance bonus component was added to that to incent the utilities to do more. That has performed well.

Outside of the investor owned utilities our municipal utilities and electric cooperatives don't have this requirement. Yet, they are still moving in that same direction.

One example, the CPS Energy which is the municipal electric and gas provider for San Antonio originally had planned to build a new 700 megawatt power plant to address future growth and load. Instead they adopted a package of efficiency measures across the service territory as well as distributed solar and some other renewable activities to achieve the same objective.

Senator FRANKEN. Mr. Clark, Mr. Rodgers, how do these standards impact your business models?

Mr. CLARK. Certainly as part of energy savings performance contracts, we've had the good fortune of implementing a number of renewable technologies for the Federal Government customers, State and local government customers including wind energy projects for a Bureau of Prisons facility in Victorville, California as well as an offshore Navy base and a considerable amount of photovoltaic or PV products both for the State of Hawaii, for example, to the Department of Accounting in General Services.

I still think, from our perspective at least, fantastic projects, fantastic components to a project, but if evaluated on a purely economic basis we still feel that's it's pretty compelling that, you know, not using energy is the most renewable form of energy all together. That efficiency on a per kilowatt/hour or per megawatt/hour investment for our customers tends to be the most cost effective solution. But certainly the renewable portfolio standards have grown that aspect of our business and have grown that portion of energy savings performance contracts.

Senator FRANKEN. Now you were talking about financing barriers. I'll go to Mr. Rodgers, but I want to talk about the barriers that you have to getting, to making sure there's finances there, for Mr. Nadel as well, is talk about how we can make sure that there is financing for these kinds of projects.

Mr. RODGERS. Mr. Chairman, in regards to the impact on companies like ours, it really begins to set the overarching, you know, standard to allow companies like ours to exist and companies like ours to assist our utility customers and our utility clients to help their customers.

A couple of things I think these standards have done is it has really brought out the best of what businesses like our do, of thinking of new and innovative ways to be able to deliver energy savings measures into the commercial, the industrial and the residential marketplace.

But one of the things, I think, that has become a challenge to our market and one that we have embraced wholeheartedly, especially in our project that I referenced in my comments on Indiana and that is of measurement and reporting. We find that there is not necessarily a consistent way of looking across the entire country at how these programs roll up and what really is the return on the investment that's being made in the marketplace. So standards like this also drive innovation through technology of really trying to take this information and the savings that is being provided to the end customers and really be able to report it in a meaningful and useable way to really bring it back to an economic discussion.

Senator FRANKEN. Is that important, Mr. Nadel, that the idea of establishing data that is that people can count on and say we know that this is what this technology does or we know this is what our savings will be?

Mr. NADEL. Having better data to better assure consumers how much they will save will be very helpful. You're not going to hit it exactly, but to very much narrow the range of uncertainty, likewise better data on the performance of projects, will be very helpful to the financiers to be able to help evaluate the risks of making different loans.

Senator FRANKEN. Therefore help to get financing and that takes me back to Mr. Clark on the barriers to getting financing.

Mr. CLARK. It's truthfully, Chairman Franken, it's a relatively new barrier. I would say that up until the point that there was the economic downturn in 2008 I think that on the State and municipal side of the equation, I don't want to say financing was abundant. But it was less of an issue.

I think today as people manage the credit rating of an entity whether it be a city or a State and in lieu of events in the city of Detroit or the city of Harrisburg where they had credit difficulties. I think it's become an increasing concern. I think one of the, or several of the things that have helped alleviate that have been the creation of these not for profit entities for the purpose of investing in energy efficiency.

I mentioned the sustainable energy utility in Delaware, the Maryland Clean Energy Commission, the Chicago Infrastructure Trust. So to the extent that these entities for investment in energy efficiency are propagated and willing and able to hold that financing that will stimulate a market and help a market get out of the condition that it has been.

I'd also say that, you know, a number of tax credits, whether it be an investment tax credit associated with investments in photovoltaic assets or new market tax credits that may be able to finance central planned assets for a design builder or build on operate projects. Certainly the continuation of and the availability of those tax credits makes it a much more cost effective transaction structure for State and local governments to do comprehensive infrastructure related energy efficiency improvements.

Senator FRANKEN. You brought up in your testimony the EPA which has indicated that it's going to engage States and stakeholders and the public to establish carbon pollution standards for existing power plants and how that could unleash projects for energy efficiency and basically as offsets. I'd like to discuss how these regulations could be crafted in such a way to do that and give States maximum flexibility to carry them out.

Anybody and I know, Mr. Clark, you have ideas on that. Commissioner Rothman.

Why don't we—we haven't heard from Commissioner Rothman in a few minutes. So let's go to him first.

Mr. ROTHMAN. Sure.

Senator FRANKEN. Give you a rest.

Mr. CLARK. Give me a rest.

Senator FRANKEN. Mr. Clark.

Mr. ROTHMAN. Of course I was a bit of a designated hitter on this topic a little bit.

First of all, Minnesota supports the efforts of Sec. 111(d) and the Administration going forward with these, with the rulemaking, wants to participate in the partnership and that dialog and has actively done so.

I'll just reference the letter that came out of my sister agency, the MPCA, pollution control on December 12, 2013 which we can submit for the record as on each of these points.

The major ones are, as you're indicating, is a topic of importance for today on energy efficiency. From our perspective in Minnesota we want to make sure that those rules have, the rule has flexibility to allow the credit for energy efficiency and renewables. Renewables should allow for definitions within each of the States. They aren't the same.

I think the key point in going back to your questioning just a minute ago, is that there needs to be key tools for data collection and measurement build in so that there can be proper credit for those kinds of offsets.

Then the last part about it that I'd like to say is that with respect to that data collection is that there needs to be, from Minnesota's perspective, an accommodation for the achievement and the successes that we've had already in the past so that Minnesota can, in essence, take credit for the opportunities we've had.

Then finally, as we note in our letter, that there needs to be some flexibility by the States with the timing. It may take more than a year to get all this in place. But we want to have that dialog.

Thank you, Mr. Chair.

Senator FRANKEN. Ah good.

Mr. Clark? Then Mr. Nadel, I know that you have a lot of thoughts about this. So we'll do that.

Mr. CLARK. Certainly agree with everything that's been said on the topic. From our perspective an energy savings performance contract in its very design is well suited to take—to both measure, verify, quantify, the CO reduction achieved in energy efficiency products done outside the utility fence. So we believe it's an excellent delivery mechanism.

Also one of the barriers at times can be the economics of an individual project or collection of energy efficiency projects. Certainly the ability to monetize a CO_2 reduction or carbon dioxide reduction over a period of time could be a catalyst or transformational in the energy efficiency market by giving another source of economics or savings stream to compel building owners to take action, you know, in cooperation and concert with a utility program.

Senator FRANKEN. Mr. Nadel.

Mr. NADEL. Yes. We believe that energy efficiency is a critical ingredient to make these Sec. 111(d) regulations on existing power plants work. It's low cost emissions savings. In fact it's savings that help reduce customer bills unlike anything else you can do.

So we do strongly support the flexibility that Mr. Rothman talked about to give States to allow them to use various mechanisms to incorporate efficiency and renewable. We think that efficiency should be considered. We need a system approach where you look what can be saved in the whole system, in the power plant itself, but also in that larger system outside including the end user to get much more emissions reductions then.

We do believe that if done right, flexible and, you know, including a lot of efficiencies, can be done in ways that will actually help the economy rather than hurt the economy. I know there's been a lot of angst here in Congress among some people that this will be a job killer or really hurt things. Yes, you could do it badly. But if you do it well and really include a strong role for efficiency we think it can actually be——

Senator FRANKEN. Unleash a lot of activity is really what Mr. Clark. We see some nodding here. Mr. Rodgers I see.

Mr. NADEL. Right. The one thing I would add is we are actually now doing a study looking at the impacts of including significant efficiency in 111(d) for each of the 50 States. We hope to have that come out at the end of March.

I know just this morning I was in a meeting where we were reviewing some of the results of Alabama. It happened to be yes. The benefits, it creates jobs. It increases State income. It looked like it could be quite positive.

Senator FRANKEN. I've been told that we have to get out of here in about 10 minutes. They're having, I think, an arena soccer game will be here a little later. We're trying to balance our budget here in Congress too and that helps, every bit helps it.

So I just wanted to ask about distributed generation and combined heat and power. This is—I'm very glad that my benchmarking amendment has been adopted by Shaheen/Portman. I like combined heat and power for a lot of different reasons.

Mr. Rothman talked about something we do in St. Paul where they have distributed energy where we really burn the biomass that's picked up from our homes in St. Paul. We burn it and it does it. It provides the electricity for St. Paul and heats and cools about 80 percent of the buildings. Right?

So Mr. Nadel, I know that you've mentioned it and if you could also encourage Mr.—or Senator Portman and Senator Shaheen maybe we can get that as part of this too.

Mr. NADEL. Yes. I mean, CHP is very important and you have a bill that would expand that to include district heating systems. We do support that. It will be a little bit challenging because there are some costs involved in trying to get bipartisan support for anything that has—costs money is challenging.

More broadly, I think much can be done by encouraging and assisting States to look at the hook up requirements in their States, look at the backup power rates to make sure that they are fair to the CHP system, to the utility and to all the other ratepayers.

Also looking at some of the environmental permitting systems. In many States they do not recognize the higher efficiency of combined heat and power. They, therefore, have overly strict emissions requirements for them.

So there are things that can be done to help encourage. Your bill is an excellent start, but there's also some other things that can be done.

Senator FRANKEN. The bill's resiliency as well. These things operate in island mode or can operate in island mode and that can, especially if you're doing things like storing important data. It's a security piece too.

Look, I just want to thank you all for your testimony. We—I know that Senator Risch is submitting some questions to the record and I might as well.

Senator FRANKEN. But I want to thank you all for the great work that you're doing. We're going to try to learn as much as we can from this and continue doing this.

But I just want to thank you for what each of you are doing in your States or around the country. I guess by now we'll adjourn this hearing.

[Whereupon, at 5 p.m., the hearing was adjourned.]

APPENDIX

RESPONSES TO ADDITIONAL QUESTIONS

RESPONSES OF MARK GLICK TO QUESTIONS FROM SENATOR MURKOWSKI

Question 1. Can you please elaborate on the Memorandum of Understanding that Hawaii signed with the Department of Energy in 2008?

Answer. The January 2008 Memorandum of Understanding (MOU) between the U.S. Department of Energy (DOE) and the State of Hawaii established the Hawaii Clean Energy Initiative (HCEI), creating a groundbreaking partnership between the state, DOE, the military and the public and private sectors. The purpose of the MOU was to forge an alliance between Hawaii and DOE that would extend to energy stakeholders and opinion leaders to pursue strategies to transform Hawaii's energy sector to achieve a target of "70 percent clean energy" by 2030. In 2009, the following targets to be achieved by 2030 were set consistent with the MOU: 1) a 4,300 GWh reduction of electrical energy consumption in the power sector as defined in the Energy Efficiency Portfolio Standard of Hawaii Revised Statutes 269-92; 2) 40 percent of Hawaii's electrical generation requirements coming from renewable resources as defined in the Renewable Portfolio Standard of Hawaii Revised Statutes 269-92; and 3) a displacement of 385,000 million gallons per year of petroleum for ground transportation as a voluntary objective of the HCEI Road Map which can be found at energy.hawaii.gov. The HCEI Road Map, which was last updated in 2011, established working groups to address key sectors of the energy economy—electricity generation, end-use efficiency, transportation and fuels. Hawaii and DOE are currently updating the MOU for execution in the second quarter of 2014 that outlines the next phase of HCEI.

Question 2. Are you meeting the goals for your Energy Efficiency Portfolio Standard (EEPS)? If so, how do you know?

Answer. The State of Hawaii is meeting the EEPS goals. One way the Hawaii State Energy Office tracks progress on EEPS is through the annual EEPS report by the Hawaii Public Utilities Commission (PUC) to the Hawaii Legislature. The most recent report in January of 2014 stated that " . . . Hawaii is on track to achieve more than 1,550 GWh in savings by 2015, exceeding the interim 2015 EEPS target of 1,375 GWh by more than 12 percent." This report can be found at http://puc.hawaii.gov/wp-content/uploads/2013/04/2013-PUC-EEPS-Report___FINAL.pdf

Another method of verification is the recent independent evaluation released by the PUC on January 15, 2014 of the energy efficiency market potential in the State of Hawaii from 2013-2030. This evaluation was conducted by EnerNOC Utility Solutions Consulting to assess whether the State is on track to meet the overall 2030 EEPS goal. From a baseline in 2012, the study presents estimates of potential electricity savings for 2013 through 2030. According to the evaluation, the projected "cost-effective cumulative energy efficiency potential to be achieved by 2030 is 6,210 GWh, or about 144 percent of the current EEPS goal.

Question 3. It seems from your testimony that you are continuing to add renewable power even though you are having grid stability issues. How are you maintaining grid stability? What do you use for base load power?

Answer. Adding high degrees of intermittent renewable generation resources safely and reliably in Hawaii has been challenging. This has necessitated recalibration of our grid reliability standards, specific technical solutions pursued by utilities, including customer-sited and grid-sited technologies to address any issues related to exceeding or increasing the current penetration threshold, and continued reliance on fossil-fueled dispatchable generation resources to assure grid stability and suitable power quality. Another challenge is the size of Hawaii's existing base-load power plants, particularly the AES coal plant and the amount of spinning reserve that must be kept running to back it up. State policy has encouraged the diversity of dispatchable renewable resources available including geothermal, waste-to-energy, biomass and biofueled generation resources. Hawaii has more than one dozen energy storage projects and the PUC may approve efforts to procure additional storage technologies and demand response resources. The utilities and the stakeholders of the Hawaii Clean Energy Initiative have leveraged federal, state and utility funding to commission studies using more sophisticated and accurate models that account for the addition of renewable energy resources and their grid impacts. Essentially, the utilities are seeking to understand to what extent conventional generators can be turned-down to allow for greater renewable energy penetration and still maintain grid stability.

Question 4. How do you partner with private sector companies and local businesses to achieve your goals?

Answer. For efficiency private sector projects, the State Energy Office partners with private lending institutions to offer low-interest loans supported by an ARRA-funded loan loss reserve.

In the renewable energy arena, the Hawaii State Energy Office reaches out to the private sector to determine which are the most pressing issues preventing renewable energy development. Once the bottlenecks are identified, we develop and deploy solutions to break-down these barriers. For example, inefficiencies in permitting processes and siting selection were determined to be major roadblocks to renewable energy development in Hawaii. Consequently, the State Energy Office pooled resources to develop the following tools to improve how developers design and deploy renewable energy projects in Hawaii:

- Renewable EnerGIS Map provides renewable energy resource and site information for specific Hawaii locations. It is intended to help landowners, developers, and policy makers understand the renewable energy potential of sites statewide.
- Renewable Energy Permitting Wizard was developed to help those proposing renewable energy projects understand the county, state and federal permits that may be required for their individual project. This tool works for projects ranging in size from residential solar installations to large utility-scale facilities. It is currently being upgraded to reflect current permitting requirements, improve user functions, and be available in an open source software environment.
- e-Permitting Portal (Department of Health) allows for the electronic processing of DOH environmental health permits.
- Permitting Guidebook provides guidance on the permitting and siting of renewable energy projects in Hawaii. Hence, it better prepares applicants for the permitting processes, which also saves time and resources for the permitting agencies and developers.
- Developer & Investor Center provides guidance and information on all facets of commercial and residential renewable energy development in Hawaii (siting, financing, utility interconnection, taxation, permitting, business registration, other opportunities).

International Agreements—The Okinawa-Hawaii Clean Energy Cooperation agreement was signed by Hawaii, the Japan Ministry of Economy, Trade and Industry (METI), the U.S. DOE, and Okinawa Prefecture to facilitate policy dialogues to share best practices and deploy joint projects in the field of renewable energy and energy efficiency including smart grids and smart city systems. Additional parties agreed to work with the principals under the framework, including the Japan New Energy and Industrial Technology Development Organization (NEDO), the Japanese Ministry of Foreign Affairs (MOFA), other related organizations and research institutions.

Among the several significant joint efforts that have emerged from this partnership is the Japan-US Smart Grid Demonstration Project. Known as JUMPSmart Maui, this innovative smart grid project is being funded primarily by NEDO using $37 million provided by Japan's Ministry of Economy, Trade and Industry. The US Department of Energy is supporting the project by providing access to their experts at three of their national laboratories (National Renewable Energy Lab, Sandia National Lab, and the Pacific Northwest National Lab). Among the many private sector partners are Hitachi, Mizuho, Maui Electric Company and Hawaiian Electric Company. This project helps Hawaii achieve R&D investment goals of the state's strategic plan for clean energy. By investigating system impacts and the means to enable increased levels of distributed generation PV, JUMPSmart Maui is a good example of Hawaii's emergence as one of the world's leading test beds for proving advanced clean energy concepts and early stage technical solutions.

57

Question 1. Please describe how a statewide approach is the best solution for Indiana but may not be for other states.

Answer. A statewide program approach, such as the Indiana statewide program, is a great fit for states that do not have strong, established and consistently defined efficiency programs that are offered by utilities in the state. Starting from the ground up enables the state to align program goals, structures and requirements seamlessly. What makes the Indiana program successful from a customer and utility perspective is that it is the same program offered to all customers across the entire state. This uniform approach can easily be applied to other states in similar situations. It is typically more challenging to modify and streamline existing programs with a longer history offered by multiple utilities into a single unified statewide approach.

Brand awareness, customer education, data management and program reporting are the clear advantages of a statewide approach. By aligning all of the individual utility goals there is synergy when it comes to program participation and overall program evaluation.

In the case of Indiana, a unique brand called "Energizing Indianar" was established for the entire suite of programs offered by all utilities. By combining all utilities under one brand, GoodCents was able to drive customer education and awareness on a much larger scale. Additionally statewide program channels allow for consistent messaging across multiple service territories which opens additional enrollment channels and the ability to leverage large scale branding campaigns to educate customers and drive increased cross selling and program participation.

Finally, offering a common program across an entire state through multiple utilities promotes economies of scale through a third-party administrator. These economies of scale include increased visibility, stronger data capture and management, and enhanced reporting capabilities across a common platform to provide information to key stakeholders. All program activities across all utilities are measured and tracked through the same process and with the same system. The requirements of program success are clearly laid out, and the data needed to back those numbers is collected and reported from the first customer interaction through the life of their participation. The unification of the program is maximized by the consistency in program implementation; data capture and ultimately program reporting.

Question 2. How have you been able to measure the success of Energizing Indiana since its beginning, three years ago? More specifically, how to you obtain tangible metrics that let you know if your efforts are really working, and how much you have saved consumers? Is it possible for you to know exactly what you are paying for? How?

Answer. As the third-party implementer for Energizing Indiana, GoodCents is required to collect, analyze and report on data from every aspect of the program. This information is then reported directly to the utilities and the Demand Side Management Coordination Committee (DSMCC). GoodCents leverages our fully integrated technology platform, GoodCents Connectr, to manage the data requirements of all programs for each participating utility. The GoodCents Connect technology platform supports all of the systems utilized in the delivery of the program and enables us to track and report on each part of the customer's lifecycle with the Energizing Indiana Program; we track each detail of the process from the time they are initially marketed through the completion of the program. This approach provides a single platform to support all program functionality and minimize the number of integrations required to share data, lessening impact to internal and external systems.

By tracking both the data and details of each program transaction we can easily measure program success by participation, transaction and deemed or measured savings. This information is presented to all program stakeholders through the Reporting Portal portion of GoodCents Connect which enables the data to be analyzed and program success and goals to be tracked in real time. The ability to continuously track a program's success and accomplishments allows us to gauge what is working and what can be improved to increase program participation or results. Unique to a consolidated statewide approach, data can be tracked and managed for all utilities in one system which allows us to easily monitor and report on the program as a whole, at any given time.

GoodCents Connect also enables us to increase our reporting ability by integrating measure level savings and reporting for improved performance accuracy. Knowing the kilowatt hours (kWh) saved by transaction, program and utility allows us to easily report and calculate total savings. By drilling both transactional and budget data down we can easily track dollars spent against program participation. This results in the capability to illustrate exactly where program dollars are being spent and the savings you are achieving for program spend.

RESPONSES OF MIKE ROTHMAN TO QUESTIONS FROM SENATOR MURKOWSKI

Question 1. How do you partner with private sector companies and local businesses to achieve your goals?

Answer. We partner with companies in three key ways to help them succeed. These partnerships inform of us of what they need to succeed (Obtain Input); allow us to tailor assistance and polices to best address those needs (Provide Technical Assistance); and connect them to financial resources best suited to help them grow (Connect to Financial Assistance).

Obtain Input

Partner with businesses to assure that our activities and policy recommendations are based on current and leading challenges and opportunities for a given sector.

- Actively participate in sector specific (energy efficiency and the production, distribution and use of renewable and non-renewable heat, power and fuel) industry meetings and events.
- Subscribe to sector specific trade journals, news services and trade associations.

Provide Technical Assistance

Partnerships are strengthened by building trust and demonstrating integrity through serving as an on-going, unbiased source of information and expertise.

- Provide one-on-one, confidential review of an energy company's innovation to best enable them to compete for funding and succeed in the market place.
- Train entrepreneurs on use of a Commercialization Milestone-based, decision making process commonly favored by DOE and DOD grant programs.
- Connect business to resources most suited to expedite development including,
  —Formal partnerships with Non-profit commercialization accelerator programs
  —DOE Clean Energy Innovation and Clean Energy Commercialization programs, and federal labs, and
  —Formal partnership with Minnesota Business First Stop—nine state agencies that synchronize assistance and leverage expertise as needed to address concerns common to innovative or complex projects today.

Connect to Financial Assistance

Strengthen partnerships through serving as a "go-to" source of information for current financial incentives and funding.

- Promote subscription to our email list server State and Federal Funding Notification Service so businesses can be informed of appropriate solicitations.
- Educate emerging companies on appropriate SBIR/STTR Programs and Venture Capital Networks.
- Educate businesses on federal and state Renewable Energy Tax Exemptions, Minnesota Energy Savings Programs and Rebates for Energy Efficiency.

Question 2. Regarding your Solar Value Tariff, how much solar power has been derived, and how is it valued (at a retail or wholesale rate)? How has the program been received by ratepayers?

Answer. Minnesota's Value of Solar tariff is still in the development phase so numbers for solar power derived are not yet available. The Department's Value of Solar Methodology is currently under review by the Minnesota Public Utilities Commission (PUC). A decision from the PUC is due by April 1, 2014. The value of solar rate is neither a retail nor wholesale rate-it is a calculation of the real value of distributed solar electricity to the utility, ratepayers, and society. We are happy to provide further details.

Question 3. In your testimony, you note "the value of energy and its delivery, generation capacity, transmission capacity, transmission and distribution line losses and environmental value." How is the term "environmental value" defined? How is it measured?

Answer. Minnesota's Value of Solar Methodology uses environmental values based on existing Minnesota and EPA environmental externality costs. CO_2 and non-CO_2 natural gas emissions factors (pounds of pollution per MM BTU of natural gas) are taken from the EPA.[1] Avoided environmental costs are based on the federal social cost of carbon values[2] and the Minnesota PUC-established externality costs for non-CO_2 emissions.[3]

Question 4. Please elaborate on Minnesota's views that the proposed Greenhouse Gas Rules for existing sources. Do you believe that Minnesota will be able to reach its own targets of a 1.5 percent reduction in energy use per year through efficiency measures and 27.5 percent generation from renewables by 2025? Why or why not? How do you believe the rulemaking can be helpful to your efforts?

Answer. Yes, we do believe that Minnesota will be able to continue to reach the goals it has set for itself.

Minnesota has required electric and gas utility companies to deliver energy efficiency to their customers since the early 1980s, but the programs have been continually strengthened. Originally, the Conservation Improvement Program, or CIP (Minnesota Statutes § 216B.241) law measured utility spending on efficiency. In 2007, the Next Generation Energy Act (NGEA) strengthened CIP to require an annual energy savings goal of 1.5 percent of retail sales for electric and natural gas utilities, one of the most aggressive standards in the country. Although individual utility performance has varied, Minnesota electric utilities collectively exceeded the 1.5 percent standard in 2011, while natural gas utilities collectively achieved the 0.75 percent and 1.0 percent minimum savings standards. In 2010, CIP projects reduced electricity consumption in Minnesota by approximately 1.3 percent out of an estimated growth rate of 2.3 percent without CIP.

Energy savings through efficiency and conservation have a sizable impact on carbon emissions. On average, each megawatt-hour (MWh) of electricity saved in Minnesota avoids 1,823 pounds (0.9 tons) of CO_2 emitted to the atmosphere, while each MCF of natural gas saved avoids 121 pounds (0.1 tons) of CO_2.[4] As a result of the electric and natural gas savings achieved through CIP in 2010-2011, nearly 2,000,000 tons of CO_2 emissions were avoided annually, equivalent to removing approximately 370,700 cars from the road for one year.[5]

In 2007, Minnesota also enacted one of the nation's most aggressive Renewable Energy Standards (RES), requiring Xcel Energy to generate at least 30 percent of its electricity from renewable energy sources such as wind, solar, and biomass by 2020, and all the state's other utilities to generate at least 25 percent of their electricity by 2025 (altogether about 27.5 percent by 2025). This is roughly equivalent to 6,000 to 7,000 megawatts of renewable capacity by 2025. All 16 utilities are on track to meet the 2012 Renewable Energy Standard (RES) benchmark goals[6] of 18 percent (Xcel) and 12 percent (all other utilities).

Most of the renewable energy generated by the RES will come from wind power. Low wind turbine prices and federal tax incentives have driven the cost of new wind generation to historically low levels and turned wind into a cost-competitive resource option. For some utilities, wind is now the least expensive option available to reliably satisfy demands for energy-even when the environmental benefits of wind power are not included.

In 2013, Minnesota adopted a solar electricity standard to obtain 1.5 percent of retail electricity sales from solar electricity by the end of 2020; this standard is in addition to the existing Renewable Energy Standard. The new law is limited to investor-owned utilities, exempting cooperative and municipal utilities. Mining and paper mills, some of Minnesota's largest electricity users, are also exempted. There is a 10 percent carve out for small scale solar photo-voltaic capacity less than 20

---

[1] See http://www.epa.gov/climatechange/ghgemissions/ind-assumptions.html and http://www.epa.gov/ttnchie1/ap42/.

[2] See http://www.epa.gov/climatechange/EPAactivities/economics/scc.html, EPA technical document appendix, May 2013.

[3] "Notice of Updated Environmental Externality Values," issued June 5, 2013, PUC docket numbers E-999/CI-93-583 and E-999/CI-00-1636.

[4] The electric CO_2 emissions rate is provided by the Minnesota Pollution Control Agency to the Minnesota Public Utilities Commission and Minnesota Department of Commerce in Docket No. E,G999/CI-00-1343 and was last updated on March 17, 2009. The gas CO_2 emissions rate of 121 pounds of CO_2 per Dth is a standard emissions factor for natural gas combustion and assumes a properly tuned boiler or furnace such that nearly 100% of fuel carbon is converted to CO_2.

[5] Calculated using the US Environmental Protection Agency's Greenhouse Gas Equivalencies Calculator (http://www.epa.gov/cleanenergy/energy-resources/calculator.html#results), accessed Feb 1, 2013.

[6] See "Progress on Compliance by Electric Utilities with the Minnesota Renewable Energy Objective and the Renewable Energy Standard," which is prepared for the Minnesota Legislature once every two years. View the full RES report and more on RES. June 1, 2013 report to Public Utilities Commission: Docket No. 13-186

kilowatts. The statute also created a goal of obtaining 10 percent of the entire state's retail electricity sales from solar electricity by 2030.

Minnesota has shown its commitment to reduce Green House Gas (GHG) emissions through its strong energy efficiency and renewable energy goals. Continued reductions will rely on the successful implementation of 111(d) rules. Recognizing that each state is responsible for the implementation of a federal program, Minnesota believes that it is important that the 111(d) program be flexible in the variety of things a state can do (plant retirements, refueling, renewable energy and energy efficiency), and that sufficient time is given (one year) to develop State 111(d) plans. Also, because of reductions that Minnesota has already achieved in emissions, it is important that past actions be taken into account when establishing the 111(d) rules.

———

RESPONSES OF WILLIAM E. TAYLOR TO QUESTIONS FROM SENATOR MURKOWSKI

Question 1. How do you partner with private sector companies and local businesses to achieve your goals?

Answer. Private sector companies and local businesses are critical partners and service providers in achieving Texas' goals of growing domestic energy resources, enhancing energy security and leveraging related economic opportunities. Specifically, our office engages private sector consulting engineers to conduct energy assessments of public facilities, which leads to energy and water saving retrofit projects financed via our LoanSTAR revolving loan program that are then implemented by local mechanical, electrical and plumbing contractors. We also provide support to emerging clean energy technology companies through a network of university-affiliated business incubators—where young companies receive professional consultation on business plans, management structure, investment strategies and technology validation.

Nationally, the 56 State and Territory Energy Offices engage private sector companies in most of their work to expand energy opportunities. This work ranges from the development of statewide energy plans created through public-private stakeholder processes to support for energy technology business incubators and demonstration projects. In addition to the state activities described in our testimony, several other examples include:

- Alaska's public facilities retrofits program includes a $250 million Alaska Energy Efficiency Revolving Loan Fund. The fund finances energy efficiency improvements linked to the benchmarking of 1,300 public facilities across the state. The benchmarking effort identifies high-energy use buildings and provides an Investment Grade Audit prior to the retrofit to help determine which improvements are needed.
- Louisiana's Home Energy Rebate Option Program works with private sector providers that link cash rebates for energy retrofits with training and quality control for the energy raters who certify the projects. This approach builds the capabilities of private sector providers to offer retrofit services to a broad range of homeowners. Over 1,100 existing homes were retrofitted, resulting in a 30 percent average increase in energy efficiency.
- Nebraska has operated the Dollar and Energy Saving Loan Program through 394 private banks for more than 22 years. The program finances energy efficient improvements in homes, farms, businesses, industrial facilities, and schools. Over 27,339 projects have been completed using more than $258.7 million in low-interest loans made through the state's participating private sector lenders. In it's more than 22 years of operation, this public-private financing program has seen defaults of only $106,000 out of the $258 million in loans.
- North Dakota operates a cost-shared training initiative implemented by North Dakota State University that helps farmers adopt conservation farming practices to lower production cost. To date, 43 workshops have been held with 861 participants.
- Ohio's Energy Efficiency Program for Manufacturers (EEPM) is a multi-phase program that provides assistance to manufacturers to diagnose, plan, and implement cost-effective energy improvements at their facilities. The state estimates ongoing savings of 28,331,432 kwh/year (electric) and 876,349 MMBTU/year (gas, oil).
- Washington has partnered with BMW and the SGL Group to launch the construction of a state-of-the-art carbon fiber automotive facility. The $100 million joint venture began in 2010. Through the development and construction stages of this process, over 200 jobs were created, and since opening, approximately 80 permanent, full-time positions have been maintained.

• Wisconsin's Smart Fleet initiative aims to evaluate government and business vehicle fleets to identify areas where they can add vehicles that run on alternative fuels like compressed natural gas. The recently launched program has evaluated 29 participating public and private vehicle fleets across the state.

In addition to working with the private sector on energy programs that expand energy opportunities and resources, the State Energy Offices also lead energy emergency planning and response, with a particular focus on liquid fuels (e.g., gasoline, propane, heating oil). There are many great examples of how states have partnered with private sector fuel and energy providers to ensure rapid restoration of services in support of health, safety, and a return to normal economic activity. The response of the Massachusetts energy office to Hurricane Sandy is a great illustration of this work. Following the hurricane the state convened a workgroup to develop "outside the box" emergency plans to ensure the state's petroleum needs were met and to assist the New York Harbor area with obtaining petroleum product. The resulting plan would allow Boston terminals to load petroleum products onto barges for shipment to New York.

Question 2. In your testimony, you describe "Green Banks," and say that Connecticut 'used $40 million to attract more than $180 million in private investment'. How exactly does that work? What is the return on investment for the private entities?

Answer. The primary strategy that states are using in the operation of "green banks" or infrastructure banks is to attract that private capital through credit enhancement mechanisms, rather than through direct lending to borrowers (although direct loans may be part of other state energy financing programs). Credit enhancements allow public funds to leverage private capital in the following ways:

• The state commits public funds to support a specific energy purpose, such as loans for home energy efficiency and renewable energy projects.
• The state solicits partner private sector financial institutions to offer loans for that purpose, using the banks' own loan application, underwriting, and payment collection processes.
• The state funds are not used directly for the loans; rather, the state funds serve the purpose of decreasing the banks' exposure to default risk. In addition, this approach can build a track record of successful bank loans in the energy efficiency area selected, which may lead to increasing amounts of private capital for loans and a diminished need for the public funds over time.

Leverage is calculated based on the ability of the public funds to increase the pool of money that is made available from the private sector for that specific type of investment. Many state financing programs do not go by the term "green bank" but have achieved up to 7:1 leverage ratios, meaning that for each public dollar used for financing, banks and credit unions have matched it with another $7 in private capital.

Credit enhancements are usually structured to fit the comfort level and return on investment expectations of the partner banks and financial institutions. Common strategies include:

• Loan loss reserve (LLR): the state establishes a fund that insures a portion of each loan against loss. Usually the LLR identifies some threshold or event that allows the bank to drawdown on the LLR fund.
• Interest rate buy-down (IRB): the state funds reduce the interest rate on the loans.
• Loan guarantee: the state puts its credit behind the loans, enabling borrowers that would typically not be considered "creditworthy" (based on FICO score, income, history of bankruptcy, business size, or other factors) to access loans or lines of credit from private banks.

The above strategies provide a subsidy, but at a far lower cost to the taxpayer than traditional grants. Importantly, they help to catalyze actions by the private sector to open new markets and fill gaps in traditional lending over time.

In addition to credit enhancements, states have been working to open a secondary market to resell these loans and achieve further leverage. For example, home energy efficiency loans in Pennsylvania and New York are structured in a "conforming" way and have a history of good performance and low defaults. This allows these states to package and sell those loans to the secondary market and use the revenues from the sales to expand the existing loan pool. NASEO has been working with the states, CITI Bank and other institutions to expand this approach. The idea is to show investors in the secondary market that these types of assets have value and can be traded.

A review of state financing programs was completed by NASEO and is available at: http://www.naseo.org/data/sites/1/documents/publications/Unlocking-Demand.pdf

Question 3. It is fair to say that the Weatherization Assistance Program (WAP) and the Low Income Heating Energy Assistance Program (LIHEAP) are helpful to low-income families with high energy bills. But, what metrics are used to ensure that this money is being used wisely? How do we know that we are getting what we pay for?

Answer. Federal regulation requires that every energy retrofit measure undertaken through the Weatherization Assistance Program (WAP) have a positive savings to investment ration, or payback, of at least $1 in energy savings for every $1 of installation. In addition, the U.S. Department of Energy's (DOE) Oak Ridge National Laboratory completed evaluation of the Weatherization Assistance Program (WAP) in 2006, which showed an average $437 average annual energy savings for each weatherized home. A new WAP evaluation is being completed and will be issued in about six months. According to DOE, preliminary results from this evaluation provide assurance that WAP continues to provide a great value for taxpayers.

In the case of LIHEAP, approximately 6.9 million of the 115 million residential households in the United States are receiving energy assistance. This is a reduction from the 8.1 million households served in 2010, due to reduced federal funding for the program. Prolonged cold weather across much of the nation this winter, as well as extraordinary spikes in propane and heating oil costs, mean that the average purchasing power of LIHEAP has declined from 47 percent of the cost of home heating to 40 percent.

The National Energy Assistance Directors Association is working closely with the U.S. Department of Health and Human Services (HHS) to develop a comprehensive program integrity plan. In addition, HHS has increased the agency's audits of the program and is in the final stages of implementing a performance measures program.

––––––––

RESPONSE OF RANDALL R. CLARK TO QUESTION FROM SENATOR MURKOWSKI

Question 1. Energy Savings Performance Contracts have a solid track record. They work to save energy and are financed by the private sector, yet they are underutilized, especially in the commercial market. In your testimony you discuss what states are trying to do to overcome some of the barriers they face. You mentioned EPA's rule, but is there a non-regulatory role for the federal government here as well? Or are these contracts best handled at the state level?

Answer. Thank you Ranking Member Murkowski for the question on how the federal government can encourage states to increase utilization of Energy Savings Performance Contracts (ESPCs).

As more states enact legislation or create programs to authorize ESPCs, the market for these contracts continues to grow. The federal government can fill gaps that exist in some state programs by improving existing national databases of energy consumption information, including the Commercial Buildings Energy Consumption Survey. To stimulate the market for purchasers and lessees of commercial buildings to utilize ESPCs, the Department of Energy could develop standardized tools and methodologies to develop an energy performance score. The scores value is to inform those states or localities enacting energy disclosure regulations and create an incentive for building owners to benchmark buildings and seek opportunities for energy savings. The federal government could also send a signal to the commercial and residential market by recognizing the value of energy efficiency investments through credit support mechanisms, such as property assessed clean energy lending and extending those programs to the commercial market.

○